THE PRIEST
&
THE PROPHET

The Christian Priest, Waraqa Ibn Nawfal's,
Profound Influence Upon Muhammad,
The Prophet of Islam

Joseph Azzi

Maurice Saliba, Translator
David Bentley, Editor

The Pen Publishers
PO Box 661336
Los Angeles, CA 90066

The Pen Publishers
P.O. Box 661336
Los Angeles, CA 90066

e-mail address waraqa@aol.com

ISBN 0-9656683 -9 -8

This book is the only authorized version to represent this writing of Joseph Azzi. The publication of this volume is not only the creative work of Joseph Azzi but also the translator, Maurice Saliba, and the editorial endeavors of Dr. David Bentley.

Printed in the United States of America

Contents

Preface

Christianity supposedly disappeared without a trace in the Arabian pennisula shortly after the emergence of the Islamic empire that overran this region by the middle of the seventh century. What this study proposes on the subject of the Christian priest, Waraqa Ibn Nawfal, is that there was a very strong case for a presence of Christians in the cities of Mecca and Medina. This presence is established by the text of the Qur'an which the unorthodox priest, Waraqa, explained to Muhammad. This took place when the priest translated the sectarian text, "The Gospel of the Hebrews."

Until recently, scholars have assigned the historical precursors of Islam to either Jewish or Christian sources. This research allows for both as Waraqa, along with many of his relatives living in Mecca, came to accept a Jewish-Christian interpretation of the revelation of Jesus Christ and of the early scriptures that proclaimed a unitarian view of God rather than a trinitarian theology.

The main object of this book is to discover the history of the Qur'an which leads us back to the simple and humble priest, Waraqa, who faithfully proclaimed an evangel for the Arabs when he translated a book designed for Jewish believers in Jesus the Messiah.

The author would like to acknowledge with his sincere thanks to Maurice Saliba who translated the original Arabic versions of "Priest and Prophet" (Qiss wa Nabi) into the French edition and from them to an English version that David Bentley has revised. Our thanks are extended to Dr. Bentley for his efforts to make this presentable for English readers. We together, extend our thanks to The Pen Publishers.

Joseph Azzi, author   **Maurice Saliba,** translator

Foreword

Christianity, Judaism and Islam are three members of the prophetic religion that claim Abraham as their father in the faith. It is natural even in this time of intermittent warfare for these three monotheistic faiths to want to discover what commonalties exists within these religions. This present book on the little known Christian relative to Muhammad leads us into the light of what Jews and Christians contributed to the Islamic faith at the beginning of the seventh Christian century.

The most amazing discovery that one can make will be the unveiling of the Qur'an's earliest sources in the other two major faiths that occupied the Arabian peninsula prior to the Islamic expansion. One cannot read the following pages without a feeling of the loss at the death of Waraqa Ibn Nawfal who left Muhammad at a critical time. The Arabic commentator simply said, "revelation dried up" for several years. However, this book will help to renew the hope that we can live together and better understand each other as "People of the Book."

The translating of the original work from Arabic to two European languages has not been without some difficulties that will appear in the quotations of the Qur'an, the Bible, and the scores of original references that are cited in the Notes. Both the Qur'an and the Bible quotations are from Joseph Azzi's own translations of these original Scriptures. He does follow the Qur'an's numbering system that is found in most English translations. Some of the verses are close to the Yusif 'Ali edition of the "The Meaning of Holy Qur'an." The Arabic, and in some cases, the French texts are cited in the Notes without much of an attempt to find English translations of these same sources even when there are English editions available.

By introducing to us the sectarian priest Waraqa, Joseph Azzi has opened a panorama of images and hopes, along with his sound handling of various facets of historical and theological information to help us look again at the complex issue of interfaith rivalries and to move us toward conciliatory understandings within this Abrahamic family.

David Bentley

"Read in the name of your Lord,
Who created man out of a mere clot
of congealed blood.
Read! For your Lord is most bountiful,
He who taught you the use of the pen
and taught man which he did not know."

Sura 96:1-6

Chapter I

Who Is Waraqa Ibn Nawfal?

Genealogy of Waraqa (560-619 AD)

Waraqa, born son of Nawfal, son of Assad, son of Abd al-'Uzzah, son of Qussayy, distant cousin to Khadijah, daughter of Khuwaylid, son of Assad, son of Abd al-'Uzzah, also son of Qussayy.

Khadijah became the first wife of Muhammad who is son of Abdallah, son of Abd al-Muttalib, son of Hashim, son of Abd Manaf, son of Qussayy.

Qussayy, the great-great-grandfather of both Waraqa and Khadijah is related to Muhammad as his great-great-great-grandfather. Waraqa, Khadijah, and Muhammad were proud members of the Quraysh clan that gained its status by its links to Qussayy, who was long celebrated as the Arab who migrated to Mecca in the middle of the fifth century. The Quraysh clan acted as one of the protectors of the holy place in central Mecca, the Ka'ba, which Qussayy helped establish as an important pilgrimage site.

Qussayy expelled the Banu-Bakr and Banu-Khuza'ah tribes from the city of Mecca to rally the scattered members of his clan, the Quraysh (the United). This is according to Ibn Ishaq (died 768), an early biographer of Muhammad and the source for Ibn Hisham's Sirah, Life of Muhammad.[1]

Qussayy managed to make a fortune and achieve fame for this tribe due to his skills of protecting water and food supplies and offering sound guidance and leadership to his impoverished people. After his death, his four children equitably shared these tasks.[2]

The following sketch reveals the structure of the Quraysh clan that begins with Qussayy.

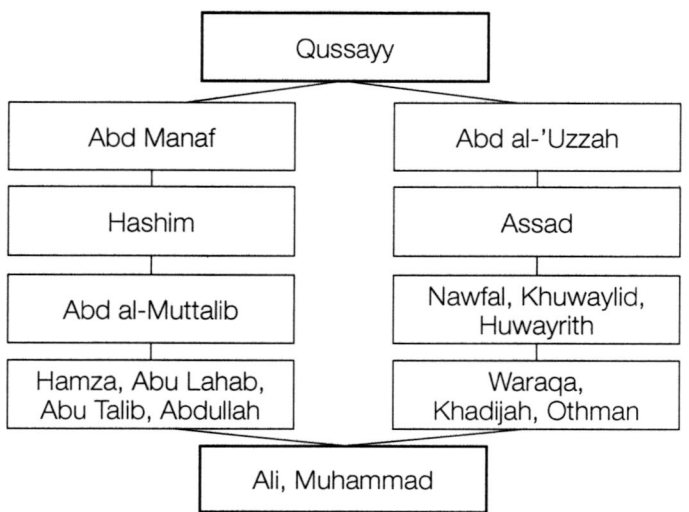

Biographical and historical documents offer numerous details on the family branch of 'Abd Manaf, whereas the branch of Abd al-'Uzzah was rarely mentioned. This is due to a definite indifference as Muhammad's multiple biographers concentrated on his branch of the descendants of Qussayy beginning with Abd Manaf. Here lies a key-point of this research which focuses on Waraqa's ancestors who are the usually ignored branch of Qussayy's family descended through Abd al-'Uzzah.

The traditional biographers' aims were to provide credibility to Muhammad's mission which meant they abandoned much that did not conform to it. Nevertheless, serious historians are required to examine all historical materials that might offer information on a specific subject. In this case, objective studies on the life of Muhammad would be better served with more attention to Abd al-'Uzzah's progeny. The reverse of this historical search has taken place as many biographers trace back to the mythological origins of selected ancestors of Muhammad, including Ishmael, Abraham and Adam.

This study provides a short history of the neglected Abd al-'Uzzah's branch leading to the significant role of Waraqa Ibn Nawfal within the Quraysh clan. The fact that there are only a few references available for covering this familial branch does not deter my interests in this subject. The preeminent contributions of Waraqa should not be rejected, as his blood relationship with Muhammad needs to be faithfully examined, along with the spiritual impact he had on the future Arab Prophet.

The important element to start with is that Waraqa, Muhammad, his wife, Khadijah, all cousins from Qussayy's Quraysh tribe, had early connections with a Meccan Christian group. This group is closely identified with the Qur'anic name, Nasorani (2:62; 5:18) that linguistically started as a general name for Christians which associates the early believers with Jesus of Nazareth. The town name not only identified Jesus but the first disciples as Nazarenes (Acts 24: 5).[3] Arab Christians assumed the name Nosrania that took on a sectarian, non-orthodox flavor. A sectarian Christian group linked up with another Christian tribe, called Banu-'Azrah, and drove Khuza'ah's clan out of Mecca and destroyed it.[4]

An important Arab source indicated that the Greek Byzantine Caesar helped the Qussayy clan to defeat the two Meccan clans, with the help a Christian allied tribe, the Ghassanids.[5] The Christian tribe of Banu-'Azrah, from the Syrian frontier area, played a mediator role between the clan of Qussayy and the Byzantines.[6] This was the first indication of the relations between Qussayy's tribe, the Quraysh, and the powerful Byzantines. Qussayy himself presented the proof that these contacts went beyond imited political alliances. He destroyed all idols in and around the Ka'ba installed by 'Amr ibn Luhayy, leader of Banu-Khuza'ah. This Yemenite tribe was the custodian of the idols inside the Meccan Ka'ba sancturay. According to an early cryptic record, Qussayy "altered the monotheist faith."[7]

Qussayy was acclaimed for the resumption of the building program for the Ka'ba. He completed its construction which was started by Tubba'h al-Yemani. Qussayy added its wooden roof. He dug out the black stone buried by the 'Ayyad tribe in the mountains of Mecca. He also emptied the area of tents to construct permanent houses which contributed to a stronger urban and pilgrimage center.

Two of Qussayy's descencants would be fascinated by their great-grandfather's productivity--the priest, Ibn Nawful, and the prophet for all Arabians, Muhammad.

Nosrania Beliefs of Waraqa

Waraqa belonged to the religion of Moses before his conversion to Nosrania.[8] He followed the monotheism of Moses as well of Jesus, i.e. the Pentateuch and the Gospel. The Qur'an repeatedly calls these monotheistic followers of Moses and Jesus, "the People of the Book." "O People of the Book! You do not have any ground to stand upon unless you stand fast by the Torah and the Gospel" (5:68). This Scripture-based belief of Waraqa is foundational to his ministry, as we shall see.

His conception of Jesus, the Christ, was less theological than that of the neighboring Najran Christians. The latter believed in Jesus' divinity. The faith of Waraqa was a sectarian heresy that survived amid constant creedal wars and outright paganism. Unlike his Jewish forebears, Waraqa and the Meccan Nosrania faithful held a high view of Jesus the promised Messiah. The Jews did not believe in the prophetic mission of Jesus Christ. When Waraqa converted to the sect of Nosrania, he accepted the belief that Jesus Christ was a prophet who came to complete the law of Moses, without assenting to the Orthodox creed that Jesus was God or son of God.

The historical records of Islam reveal that in this Hijaz area of central Arabia there were several groups of Arabs who embraced the Nosrania faith. Included among the individual converts were some members of the Quraysh tribe. Standing out on this list is Abd al-'Uzzah, son of Qussayy. The historian al-Ya'qubi alludes to this fact by writing, "Among Arabs converted to Nosrania, there are a group of Quraysh, of Banu-Assad son of Abd al-'Uzzah, and Waraqa, son of Nawfal, son of Assad."[9]

The same historian described the religious affiliation of the Meccan non-Christians. "Regarding the religion, the Arabs were divided in two groups: al-Hums (the zealous) and al-Hillah (the indifferent). The Quraysh belongs to the first group."[10] Al-Ya'qubi went on to explain the Arab religious practices relating to the Quraysh clans.

"In general Banu-Quraysh and the descendants of Mu'ad, son of 'Adnan, in particular, professed the creed of Abraham, undertook the pilgrimage, constructed hermitages, preached to the foreigners, respected the holy month, denounced obscenities and punished crimes. They behave always as if they were the masters of these places."[11]

Another historian, Al-Azraqi (d. 837), studied evidence of the Nosrania churches among the Quraysh by noting archeological excavations. "They set up in the al-Ka'ba images of prophets, trees and angels. One could see those of Abraham, Jesus, son of Mary, and angels." Following the 632 AD "conquest of Mecca, Muhammad came into the sanctuary. He sent al-Fadl, son of al-'Abbas, son of 'Abd al-Muttalib, to bring him water from the spring Zamzam. He asked for a piece of coarse cloth and ordered to wet it in that water to sponge out all images. However, Muhammad placed his hands on those images of Jesus son of Mary, and says, 'Wipe out all these images except those under my hands.'"[12]

Modern map of Arabian Peninsula

Conversion of Arab Tribes

Historians and biographers mention the conversion of manifold Arab tribes to either Orthodox or sectarian Christianity. According to Ibn Qutayba: "Nazarene influence extended among the tribes of Rabi'ah Ghassan and Quda'ah." The historian al-Ya'qubi records the conversion to this religion the following tribes: "Rabi'ah, Banu-Taghlib, Tay'h, Mazhaj, Bahra', Sulaykh, Tannukh and Lakhm."[13] Also, al-Jahiz (nickname of the writer Abu 'Uthman 'Amr ibn Bahr, who died 869), was aware of this phenomenon. He noted, "The Nazarene creed penetrated a good way among the tribes of Taghlib, Shiban, 'Abd al-Qays, Quda'a, Sulaykh, al-'Ibad, Tannukh, Lakhm, 'Amilah, Juzzan, Kuthayyir bin Bilharith bin Ka'b."[14] These references and those mentioned by other Compilers testified that the Nosrania was present in Mecca, in the surrounding Hijaz, and other areas of the Arab hinterlands as well as in southern Syria.[15]

Nosrania entered Mecca through 'Abd Manaf's and 'Abd al-'Uzzah's branches of the Quraysh tribe. This is validated by other biographers who unfortunately hesitate between two alternatives--either the recognition of the prophet's monotheistic ancestors or the sensual embellishment of raw pre-Islamic paganism and polytheism. Al-Mas'udi, one of the best-known Arab geographers and historians (d. 956), inclined toward the first option.[16]

Al-Isfahani, an Arab literary historian (d. 967), referred to Waraqa as al-Qiss, a title for a holy man among the Christians. He noted, "Al-Qiss Waraqa was one of those who gave up idolatry in the period of ignorance prior to Islam (Jahiliyya). He sought a holy religion, read holy books and abstained from eating the pagan meat."[17] The ninth century historian, Ibn Sa'd added, "Al-Qiss Waraqa was one of four persons who gave up idolatry, certain meats--that of strangled animals, and animal blood."[18]

The three other Arabs identified by Ibn Hisham as followers of the Christian sect were (1) 'Ubayd Allah, ibn Jahsh, ibn Umaymah, ibn 'Abd al-Muttalib, who died in Ethiopia as a Nosrania believer. His wife, Umm Habiba, was married later to Muhammad.[19] (2) 'Uthman ibn al-Huwayrith, a cousin of Waraqa and Khadijah, daughter of Khuwaylid and Muhammad's first wife. He became a Christian in an area dominated by the Byzantines. He enjoyed certain notoriety when a Caesar called al-Batriq imprisoned him in Damascus where he died.[20] (3) Zayd ibn 'Amr ibn Nufayl, of whom the prophet said: "Alone he is able to resuscitate a nation."[21] He was al-Khattab's nephew. His fame was great because "he prohibited killing maids buried alive."[22]

These individuals were descended from Abd al-'Uzzah and Abd Manaf's branches of the Quraysh. They become well known because of their conversion to Nosrania faith and their respect for all obligations imposed by the Apostolic Council of Jerusalem held in the year 49 AD (Acts 15:24-30). The obligations were "to abstain from touching the stains of idols, to refrain from sexual immorality, to abstain from eating blood-drained meat and animal blood" (Acts 21:25). Equally, they respected the law of Moses, the Gospel of Jesus, and the rites of circumcision and baptism.

However, there were specific Nosrania practices of the priest Waraqa and his three companions that did not agree with the recommendations of the Jerusalem Council attributed to the apostle James. The later creeds settled on the faith in Jesus Christ as Son of God and in his crucifixion and in his resurrection according to the four canonical gospels. The sectarianism of Waraqa and his colleagues rejected the divinity of Jesus Christ and some went as far as questioning the crucifixion and resurrection of Jesus. This creed corresponded to that of a well-known Nazarean sect, called Ebionism, to which belonged Waraqa and a large number of his fellow Quraysh tribesmen.

Ebionism of Waraqa

Nosrania Christians originated from a Jewish system of beliefs and practices before they settled in Mecca and the Hijaz. Their beliefs divided them into sects and parties. The Qur'an accounts for these divisions: "Parties have, among themselves, different views" (43:65). According to the Qur'an, "they are divided into sects. Each party sticks to his belief" (30:32).

Muhammad, while still a novice, developed a long-term fear of any disunity among those who advocated the oneness of God. He refused to become a member of one of these sects because he saw it sowing seeds of disputes. "I was afraid that you ask me later, 'Why did you sow the seeds of discord among children of Israel?'" (20:94). He wished them peace while hoping to bring unity among them. "We do not put any difference among them. We are resigned to God's will" (2:136; 3:84). Regarding his own followers, he says, "they believe in God and in his apostles and they do not do any difference among them" (4:152). Muhammad's expressed view is that the faithful in each party "believe in God, in his angels, in his book and in his messengers. They say: 'we do not do any difference among his apostles'" (2:285).

Along with the testimony of the Qur'an, it is important to look at other documents that were available at the beginning of the seventh century. In this critical time, ecclesiastical history identified some specific Jewish-Christian sects and their teachings. The most famous of these were Ebionism, Cerinthism and Elkasaism.

Ebionism

This sect represented the faith of a Jewish Nazarene group. Its adherents followed Jesus the Messiah and considered him a great prophet among the prophets. They believed neither in his divinity nor in his divine sonship. He was a man like all men. He received the revelation after his baptism by John the Baptist. They believed that the Christ, as an eternal principle, became incarnate in Jesus on the day of his baptism. But this left him on the day of his martyrdom.[23]

Ebionists recognized a single, noncanonical gospel. They called it the Gospel of Hebrews. It also is called the Gospel of Matthew, but an "unachieved, distorted and falsified one," according to Epiphanius.[24] They believed in constant body washing for ablutions and purification. They abstained from meat eating. They stressed medical and welfare work by serving orphans, poor people and travelers. Harboring the destitute, giving food to the hungry and welcoming foreign travelers were part of their duties. The name of this group indicated a close association with Jesus' words, "Blessed are the poor" (Matthew 5:3) This beatitude translated in their Hebraic language: "Blessed are the Ebionists."[25]

Ebionism According to Epiphanius

"For Ebion said that Jesus was generated by sexual intercourse and the seed of Joseph...
He was attached to Judaism's Law of the Sabbath, circumcision and Samaritan observances...
He added the rule about care in touching a gentile.... He repudiates celibacy and continence altogether." (Panarion 120, 121)

Irenaeus in his work "Against Heresies,"[26] Origen in "Against Cel II"[27] and Epiphanius in his *Panarion* alluded to this sect. Supposedly some monks of the Qumran, Dead Sea Scrolls community, joined this sect after the destruction of Jerusalem's Temple. They immigrated to Hijaz area where other Arab tribes merged into this sect.[28]

Cerinthism

The founder of this sect is Cerinthus. He stipulated that the heavenly kingdom of Christ is like the earthly one. He taught that the role of Jesus the Messiah consisted in liberating his people from Roman, as well as other foreign occupations. His mission was political and social. Further, heavenly paradise is designed to give satisfaction to human bodies. Eusebius who quoted Cerinthus noted, "As he loved his own body, especially in that he was by nature sensual, he believed that this kingdom would lead to all the pleasures that he coveted, namely food, drinks and carnal delights."[29]

Elkasaism

The name of this sect was based on its Arab founder, Elkasai. His followers were called "people of science." According to the beliefs of this sect, Jesus Christ should be a human being like all men.[30] The Christ personage was separated from Jesus before his martyrdom. As for the Holy Spirit, he could be either Christ's mother, a feminine being, or Gabriel the Archangel, a masculine being. Elkasai claimed that Gabriel had brought him from heaven with "the well preserved book in a holy frame."[31] He learned from Gabriel the mysteries of wisdom and metaphysics.

Some studies of religion of the first centuries of Islam have found a correspondence between the sectarian ideas of Nosrania and the teachings of the Qur'an. Such topics like the refutation of Christ's divinity, his honor as a great prophet, the questions surrounding his crucifixion were found in the Christian sects and in the Qur'an. Both were informed of these theological differences because of their mutual presence in Mecca.

The Science, 'Ilm, of Religious Knowledge

Waraqa's acquired "science" that emphasizes his broad knowledge, his regular learning of the holy books, is drawn from the "People of the Book", i.e. from those who accepted the Pentateuch and the Gospel, and by other Christian sects. These are described in the Qur'an as "the strong in science, 'Ilm- knowledge of holy things"

(4:162), "men talented in science" (3:18), "who know well the holy book" (10:94), and "a witness with a knowledge of the book" (13:43).

Knowledge had a place of honor for both the intellectual reasoning of the earlier Gnostics and the mysticism of Elkasaism's disciples. Knowledge extended to a wide breath of human experiences that included emotional and physical states. In Mecca, the monks could be seen in a state of piety and meditation with tears in eyes. The Qur'an reflected on these Christian monks, "You will see their eyes overflowing with tears when they recognize the truth" (5:83). Their science lies in the entire knowledge of the holy books. "They have received the scriptures and knew it as they knew their own children" (2:146; 6:20).

Regarding the connoisseurs of knowledge (al-A'raf), they are men who know well all people and their complexities. They are able to scrutinize what is hidden and mysterious. "Those who will stay at al-A'raf (heights) of knowledge will know every one by his (facial) marks" (7:46).

"God will raise up to suitable ranks and degrees, those of you who believe and who have been granted knowledge" (58:11). These elevated ones will enjoy the sciences which they have at their disposal. "For when their apostles came to them with clear signs, they exalted in such science they own" (40:83). They appreciate what God has given them as truth. "And those to whom knowledge has come, see that the revelation sent down to you from your Lord, that is the truth" (34:6). They observe the book of God and meditate on it alone without any other book. "He will say to those endued with knowledge and faith, 'Indeed you did not limit God's decree'" (30:56). For the possessors of science this book contains convincing evidences. "Here are signs self-evident in the hearts of those endowed with knowledge" (29:49).

These masters of the science of knowledge testify with God and the angels, the truth of Islam and Muhammad's mission. "God gave this witness... the angels and those endued with knowledge, standing firm on justice... the religion before God is Islam" (3:18, 19). Their testimony is sufficient: "Say: Enough for a witness between you and me is God and those who have knowledge of the book" (13:43). The people of science, so speaks the Qur'an, are the believers who submitted to the one God. "Knowledge was bestowed on us in advance of this, and we have submitted to God in Islam" (27:42). They have believed in the Qur'an before all other believers. "Those who are firmly grounded in knowledge say: We believe in the book; the whole of it is from our Lord" (3:7). "Those among them who are well-grounded in knowledge, and the believers believe in what has been revealed" (4:162).

This kind of esoteric knowledge is not uncommon for monks and priests of the desert areas. Homilies of the monk Ibn Sa'ida are well known in Arab literature. Another famous monk, Buhayra, or Bahira, whom Muhammad met during his caravans to Syria, was highly beloved by the Quraysh. One said about him: "The knowledge of Nazarenes reached him speedily."[32] The monk, 'Addass of Ninive "transmitted to Muhammad his knowledge on the Book."[33] A second, Syrian monk, 'Issah, said, "God grants him plenty of this special knowledge."[34] Muhammad knew another monk from 'Ukaz who was qualified in the healing arts. He went to him with his grandfather, Abd al-Muttalib, to get medical treatment for his eye disease.[35]

Within this framework of knowledge, Waraqa seems to be cognizant of the Gnostic sectarians of the Arabian desert. He becomes the expert, the interpreter of the Divine will, the sublime teacher. He explains the content of the holy books, preaches its teachings, and practices its duties, while illuminating its mysteries. He emerges as the wise expert described in the Qur'an. "*ALR.* This book, whose verses are steadily written and developed, comes from the wise, the well-versed (in all things)" (11: 1).[36]

Waraqa Translator of Scriptures

"The monk Waraqa wrote the Hebrew book. He wrote from the Hebrew Gospel what God desired." (Al-Bukhari, died 870. "Sahih," as explained by al-Karmani, Vol. I, p. 38,39.)

"The monk Waraqa wrote the Arabic book. He wrote from the Gospel in Arabic what God liked to be written." (Muslim, died 875, "Sahih," Vol. I, p. 78, 79).

"Waraqa converted to Nosrania during the Jahiliyya 'period of ignorance.' He wrote the Hebrew book. He wrote from the Hebrew Gospel what he liked to write." (Abu al-Faraj al-Isfahani, "Kitab al-Aghani," Vol. III, p. 114.)

The Mission of Waraqa

Since the Nosrania Meccans already knew the Hebrew Gospel at his disposal, Waraqa would devote much of his time putting this Gospel into Arabic. In addition to his local Arabic language, Waraqa knew Aramaic, the prevailing regional language and Hebrew, the Jews' religious language. All were used in his translation of the sacred text.

The Hebrew Gospel was recognized by several early church fathers of the Greek and Latin worlds. It was widely dispersed among Nazarean communities in the Eastern churches. St. Jerome (d. 419) found this Scripture in Aleppo. He translated it from Aramaic into Latin.[37] Ignatius of Antioch who was martyred in 107 referred to it.[38] So did Origen in Alexandria in the middle of the third century.[39]

One never finds in the Qur'an the word "Gospels" - the plural form, whereas other official or apocryphal gospels existed and were known since the first century of Christendom. The Christians knew the Gospels of Matthew, Mark, Luke and John. As far back as the beginning of the Christian era, Nazareans knew the Gospel of Peter, the Gospel of Twelve Apostles, the gospel of Nazarenes, the Gospel of Childhood of Jesus, as well as that of the Hebrews.

The single Gospel of the Qur'an appears to be the Hebrew Gospel. There is widespread agreement between it and the Qur'an in matters such as duties, prayers and resurrection. The Qur'an considers the Hebrew Gospel as God's message to Jesus, son of Mary. "He sent down the Pentateuch and the Gospel" (3:3). "We sent in their footsteps Jesus, son of Mary, to whom we gave the Gospel" (57:27). The Qur'an recalls parables similar to those found in the Ebionite Gospel: "Thus they are described in the Torah and in the Gospel: they are like a seed which sends forth its blade" (48:29).

The Qur'an calls for a witness to give evidence of the prophet's mission. "That what they find [is] quoted in their books: the Pentateuch and the Gospel" (7:157). The believers in the Gospel are directed to the Qur'an's frankness. "That the Gospel's people appreciate what God sent down in the former revelation" (5:47).

In its own way, the Qur'an exposes the only gospel, which Waraqa translated into Arabic during the first decades of the seventh Christian century. It is the gospel that the Ebionists used. However, in the surrounding regions of Mecca, other gospels and other Nazarene books were in circulation among the Christian sects in central Arabia.

Al-Qiss Waraqa, as the leader of the Nosrania Church of Mecca, assumed responsibilities for instruction, exegesis and interpretation of scriptures. He had to explain the Gospel to his kinsmen who were largely ignorant of spiritual matters. This led him to the Hebrew Gospel, the Matthew book, to translate it in a clear, accessible Arabic language. While he was deemed first among them, their master, their head and their tutor, he assumed his pastoral role with humility. Surrounding Waraqa were a number of gifted Quraysh tribesmen, who included his grandfather, Abd al-Muttalib, recognized as "lord of Mecca." Other notables were Abu Bakr al-Siddiq, 'Uthman, ibn al-Huwayrith, Zayd ibn Nufayl, 'Ubayd Allah ibn Jahsh, 'Abdallah ibn Jad'ar as well as some others who were known for their asceticism and devotion in Mount Hara'. To this list of mighty men will be added the name of Muhammad who served with Waraqa for forty-four years.

The tasks that the Ebionite priest assumed were increasingly augmented by the attention that Waraqa gave to Muhammad. He married him to Khadijah. He initiated him to prayer and meditation on Mount Hara'. He announced his prophecy to his fellow Arabs in Mecca. All his other tasks as a Meccan authority in matters spiritual and temporal were secondary as Waraqa and Muhammad attached themselves to each other to reach a common goal. Later, certain writers and authors of Muhammad's life in the Sahih and Hadith literature recognized the unique role of the monk and the prophet together. Al-Bukhari wrote, 'Since Waraqa's death, revelation dried up."[40] Muhammad's view of Waraqa's death is highly meaningful.

"I saw him in the center of Paradise. He was wrapped in a white shroud. I perceived for him one or two paradises."[41]

Death of Waraqa

Very little information is available on Waraqa's death. According to various testimonies, the priest Waraqa would be more than one hundred years old at the time of his death. Longevity was not unknown in those areas, as Abd al-Muttalib, grandfather of Muhammad, could have died over a hundred years old. Waraqa's death took place three or four years after the beginning of Muhammad's mission when he was forty-four years old. This agrees with Ibn al-Jaouzi's quotation in the "Book of Pleasure." "Waraqa is dead in the fourth year of the mission."[42] This information is repeatedly confirmed in Ibn Ishaq's "Biography of the Prophet" as well as in the "Book of Khamis."[43]

The impact of Waraqa's death was recognized by al-Bukhari's quotation: "Waraqa was scarcely dead, then the revelation became lukewarm."[44] This underlines the prominent role Waraqa played in Muhammad's mission. He was his faithful upholder, the wise guide and the sure mediator between him and God.

Later commentators, Muslim and non-Muslims, are not unanimous about the faith of Waraqa at his death. Did he die a Muslim or sectarian Christian--Nazarene? According to Ibn al-'Abbas, "he is dead in conformity with his Nazarean creed."[45] But Ibn al-Jaouzi stressed, "The priest, al-Qiss Waraqa is dead in al-Fatra and is buried in al-Hojoun. He was not Muslim."[46] Al-Fatra is the historical period between Jesus and Muhammad, i.e. the time without any prophecy. Al-Hojoun is the cemetery of believers in One God (al-Hunafa') from Qurayshi tribes. Abd al-Muttalib, Muhammad's grandfather and parents are buried there.

Muhammad's vision of Waraqa in paradise is challenged by another vision of Waraqa in one of the hadiths. "I saw Waraqa in paradise. He is dressed in silk. I perceived him in the bottom of paradise, wrapped by a shroud." He adds later, "I saw him again. I saw a white dress on him. I believe if he was among the people of hell, he would not wear such a white dress."[47]

If most of the reports do not confirm the message of Waraqa, they testify at least to his resilient faith that grants him his place in paradise. Some historians, who said that he was dead in conformity with his Nazarean faith, perhaps wished his condemnation much more than his redemption. Waraqa made acquaintance with Muhammad's mission without believing in it or being converted to Islam.

Compilers of Muhammad's Sirahs provide very few facts on the priest Waraqa aside from his humble origins with the dominant Quraysh tribe, his leadership, and his active mission in Mecca.

These scarce historical facts should be weighty because the Qur'an confirms their existence. In fact, most of the Qur'anic teachings could not be understood if the teachings of the early Hebrew Gospel were unknown. Also, it will be difficult to understand the history of the Old Testament prophets or the teachings of the Pentateuch or the Gospel, as they are given in the Qur'an, if they are not found in the original framework from which they have been drawn. The story of John, son of Zecharian, the angel's announcing John and Jesus' birth, Jesus' miracles, and his gospel message, all of these had an impact on Muhammad's mission that ncluded these salient features inscribed in the Qur'an.

In all cases, it will be difficult to understand the continuity of revelation granted tc prophets and the transmission of teaching, stories and laws given by various individuals, without the presence of a qualified scholar able to guide this continuity. Consequently, he must be the mediator between prior and post revelations, i.e. between the Pentateuch and the Gospel on one side, and the Arabic Qur'an on the other.

Chapter II

Good Relations
Between Waraqa and Muhammad

Waraqa Performs Muhammad's Marriage

Abu Talib, protector and paternal uncle of Muhammad, urges his nephew to find a livelihood as Muhammad appeared to be bound to poverty. "My nephew," he told him, "I am a man without fortune. We own neither money nor business to support ourselves."[1] Some days later, the young man finds a job as caravaneer in the business of Khadijah, who is a widow and also a first cousin to the monk Waraqa. She inherited from her second husband a transport caravan business that transversed between Arabia and Syria. Muhammad works honestly and faithfully in that business. Khadijah remunerates him double that of other salaried employees from her clan.[2]

One day Khadijah sends her servant, Nafissah, to Muhammad to discuss marriage with him. This servant gives the following account on the meeting: "Khadijah sent me discreetly to meet Muhammad who was returning from a caravan trip to Syria (Bilad al-Sham). The servant approaches the twenty-five year old Muhammad and asks, "Why do you not get married?" Muhammad responds, "Why? I do not own anything." Nafissah answers, "And if she confers on you all and gratifies you with money, beauty, honor and makes you comfortable and autonomous, what will you say?"

"Who is she?" He asks instantly.

"Khadijah!"

"Is it possible?" He asks with wonderment.

"Of course, I'll see to it."

Nafissah reports later, "I returned directly to see Khadijah and told her what happened. Immediately she sends him a messenger to arrange a meeting."[3] Most of the same Compilers that record the above conversation go on to write about the events leading to the wedding of Muhammad with his distant cousin Khadijah. This begins when Khadijah arrives with her uncles and Muhammad came with his own entourage. In the presence of this assembly, Abu Talib proclaims, "My nephew intends to marry Khadijah, daughter of Khuwaylid, and she also has the same intention to marry Muhammad."

Then the priest Waraqa, protector of Khadijah, proclaims at once, "Let us give thanks to God who created and favors us. We are lords and heads of the Arabs and you are their relatives. The Arabs will never forget your worthiness. O people of Quraysh! Let us be witnesses. I marry Khadijah, daughter of Khuwaylid, to Muhammad, son of Abdallah."

Greatly delighted and deeply relieved, Abu Talib raises his voice, "Let us give thanks to God who delivers us from sadness and dispels our worries."[4] Then he adds this statement about his nephew, "I swear by the name of God! Following this marriage he will make a great revelation and assume a dangerous role."[5] This marriage is an important event in the life of Waraqa and Muhammad. It is also important for Abu Talib to be released from the guardianship of his nephew. Muhammad begins hearing voices announcing his future prophetic mission shortly after the wedding. The Compilers of the Sirah biographical and historical documents widely recall the role of Waraqa as a role that was according to God's will.

The Significance of the Marriage

First of all the status of Waraqa must be emphasized by Muhammad's marriage to Khadijah. Al-Qiss Waraqa is among the masters and heads of the Meccan community. He confirms this status in the wedding ceremony when he proclaims: "We lords and heads of the Arabs." His Arab relatives consider him the spiritual leader and a manager within the Nosrania community. Indeed, he not only presides at the wedding ceremony but also fulfills a primacy position over all of those present at this special wedding.

Secondly, it is important to mention that Waraqa himself celebrates the marriage by establishing the contract that is publicly proclaimed. He is the main officiant--priest-pastor, who in the name of God establishes a contract from which a man can only be released at the death of a partner according to Ebionist teachings of the Gospel. As the Nosrania-Christian clergyman, he consecrates the union of his two cousins, Muhammad and Khadijah.

Muhammad's Wedding Contract

The form of the marriage contract announced by Waraqa in presence of the bridegroom, the bride and the public present is detailed in Ibn Hisham "Life of Muhammad."[6] It includes some basic elements which confirm the validity of the marriage:

The presence of a Qiss and his patronage. This is perceptible in the expression, "I marry" and then names the couple to be married.

The agreement of the bridegroom and the bride has been repeatedly confirmed by Nafssah narrating the consent of Khadijah by saying to Muhammad: "I have a desire for you," which produces an immediate response from Muhammad.[7] Abu Talib announces the desire of his nephew toward Khadijah.

The presence of eyewitnesses who are from the Quraysh clan and close family relatives.

The priest officiant announces the marriage contract.

The marriage's continuity that unites the married couple until the death of one of them.[8]

Thirdly, Waraqa's hopes for his clan in union with Khadijah can now be underscored. Waraqa himself arranges the marriage and is the first to announce it. "Our wish," he claims, "lies in establishing a tie of your line and your honor."[9] Khadijah's father who opposed this marriage once cried out, "May I let her get married to the orphan of Abu Talib? Never! Out of the question!" But Khadijah insists, "Father! Aren't you ashamed of speaking so! Do you like to humble yourself in front of the Quraysh?" She persists until he gives his consent.[10]

In another narration Khadijah is reported to have said to Muhammad: "Go and see your uncle and ask him to join us tomorrow." Upon his arrival she tells him, "Abu Talib! Go and see my cousin, Waraqa, and ask him to marry me to your nephew, Muhammad, son of Abdallah." Abu Talib replies, "Khadijah! Don't commit such an unseemly deed." But she answers, "This is God's plan." Abu Talib went to her cousin with ten members of his family soon after that meeting.[11] It is still too early to understand the plan of Waraqa. What is he looking for? As an Ebionist clergy is he strictly looking for protection of the orphan and impoverished Muhammad? Or is he looking for his own successor as a leader and lord among the Quraysh's clan?

Fourthly, the participation of Abu Talib in the priest's plan should be noted. Did not the uncle proclaim solemnly during the wedding ceremony? "I swear by the name of God! Following this marriage my nephew will have a great revelation and will assume a dangerous role." How is Abu Talib able to know the future destiny of his nephew?

After his uncle's assent, Muhammad marries the twice-widowed Khadijah. Abu Talib bestows a blessing upon all those at this Meccan wedding. "Let us give thanks to God who delivers us from sadness and dispels our worries!" This declaration leads also to other questions.

Was Muhammad a burden for his uncle? The two were close. "He never did sleep other than near him. Until his death, Abu Talib did not stop protecting, guiding and supporting his adopted nephew."[12] How should he accept all these changes? Is not the uncle relying on the priest's plan for Muhammad? Did not the aged Abu Talib see something more important on the horizon for Muhammad as he would be assuming spiritual leadership and a temporal authority among the Arabs under the guidance of fellow clan member, Waraqa Ibn Nawfal?

At the end, Muhammad appears to complete Waraqa's mission with the Meccan Nosrania believers. He is married to a woman some fifteen years his senior and mother of two children.[13] However, audacious as he was, he would never think of himself as a servant or employee. In the first instances, perhaps with pity, she hires him for her transport business. Other men from her clan undoubtedly sought her, but she refuses all. Even with the love that existed between them, Muhammad would not have her as spouse without an arrangement conducted by a powerful and influential member of the Quraysh clan. Can that individual be none other than the priest Waraqa? Indeed, without him, all could be a loss for Muhammad.

Waraqa Tutors Muhammad

From now on Muhammad's destiny depends on Khadijah and vice versa. Numerous problems have been resolved in Waraqa's plan for the marriage. Waraqa puts all his experiences at Muhammad's disposal and points him toward a promising future. From her own wifely position, Khadijah, the wealthiest lady of Quraysh, is doing what is in her power to facilitate the realization of her cousin, Waraqa's, wishes. Waraqa and Khadijah cooperate together to prepare Muhammad for his mission. This requires a continuous tutelage with a particular spiritual emphasis.

The first step Muhammac takes is the withdrawal to Mount Hara'. There he will practice ascetic devotions. His grandfather usually traveled to that place with his Quraysh companions for the same purposes. Waraqa and Muhammad seek solitude and withdraw to a cave in this area where they will spend one month each year and during fasting times over a fifteen-year period. In this cave retreat, Khalwah, Waraqa, good practitioner of divine and human affairs, instructs Muhammad.

This type of withdrawal is not strange for Muhammad. He knew it since his early youth according to his relatives' personal observations. His foster-mother, Halima al-Sa'diuuah, reports:

"In growing up Muhammad went out sometimes with his peers. As soon as they started playing, he left them and went to an isolated place. When he begins to assume his mission, his love for the Khalwah increased. For Muhammad, this contemplation liberated the heart and the spirit from all the world's attractions for a life in God's presence". The Halima report goes on, "In the Khalwah the light of knowledge illuminates the dark cave. Nothing is more important for him than to be alone and meditate on God. He usually did so on Mount Hara' where he practiced days and nights of meditations."[14]

Later a favorite wife, Aishah, spoke about Muhammad's retreats. "He was terribly keen on devotions. He cuts himself off on Mount Hara' where he practices asceticism.[15] Then he comes back to his family. He returns to Khadijah to get provisions." During her lifetime, Khadijah confirms these episodes. "God provided him the love of the Khalwah in which the heart can be liberated from all the world's preoccupations."[16]

However, Muhammad would not be able to appreciate his soul's purification if he had not met others who had experienced these intense devotions before him. The future prophet follows the religious exercises of his grandfather, Abd al-Muttalib, and his companions, like Abu Umayyah Ibn al-Mughirah, the priest Waraqa and others.[17] Muhammad adopts their example preparing his inner life for his public mission.

Among Muhammad's biographers who mention his Khalwah cave is al-Ya'qubi, who Ibn Hisham records, "The messenger of God settled himself in Mount Hara' one month per year. So did also other members of Quraysh clan during Jahiliyyah time."[18] Another Compiler gives further details. "The messenger of God settled himself in Mount Hara' one month per year. He provides food to the poor who came to see him. At the end of that month, he returns to the Ka'ba before reaching home. He circles it seven times and heads home."[19]

What specifically took place on Mount Hara' is not fully known. The Compiler, al-Balquini, who interprets al-Bukhari is quoted: "Nothing is mentioned in the Hadith we know about the procedure of his devotions."[20] What descriptions we have of these ascetic practices agree that there were similar practices between Nosrania and other Christian traditions of that time.

Asceticism and Withdrawal

Retirement to secluded places means giving up human passions to meet God with clean hands and a clean soul. The setting on Mount Hara' avoids all disputes and keeps one far from worldly worries. One seeks God in a state where the "heart is liberated from earthly problems and allows for the extended recitation of God's name. In the solitude, lights of knowledge illuminate and enlighten.[21] Disciples would spend their time in meditation, penance and listening to sermons about God's words in revealed books. Competent guides like Waraqa, offered instructions to Muhammad and others. "Before the arrival of the prophecy, Muhammad practiced his devotions according to Abraham's and Moses' laws, or to other laws and traditions prevailing at that time."[22]

The same Sirah says, "Muhammad practiced fasting like Moses and Elijah on Mount Horeb (Exodus 3:1) and like Jesus and the first Christian Fathers in the deserted places in Palestine. Muhammad and others spent the month eating only one meal per day. They satisfy themselves by partaking light food of local herbs, fruits, dairy products, bread and plants. The intention for eating is for reducing only hunger and for satisfying his elementary nutritive needs."[23]

Muhammad's Khalwah prompts him to reach out to the destitute. "He gave food to the poor who came to see him."[24] Birds and the mountain's wild beasts benefited from his kindness. Because

Muhammad himself suffered from deprivation since early childhood, he practices charity toward the poor who cross his path. From his grandfather, his uncle and his cousin Waraqa he learns to be charitable and generous toward the uncer-privileged. In his teachings he urges people to give alms, to care for widows, orphans and travelers. He rarely criticizes the opulent and intolerant classes among the Meccans.

Ramadan's month of fasting has pre-Islamic occurrences. This is the month of fasting and special prayers. Muhammad spent it in Mount Hara' where he contemplated God and holy books. Ever before the introduction of Qur'anic legislation, Ramadan was a fasting month for Nosrania believers, as mentioned in the Qur'an. "O believers! Fasting is prescribed to you as it was prescribed to those coming before you"(2:183).

At the end of the fasting month, Muhammad comes down from Mount Hara'. He typically goes first to the Ka'ba to offer thanks and later to the feast marking the close of Ramadan. According to the Compilers, at the end of Ramadan, he returns to circle the Ka'ba seven times.[25] Christians who, following their Lenten fasting, celebrated by encircling their churches seven times on Palm Sunday first practiced circling a holy sanctuary. Other religious practices that Muhammad adopts are far more difficult than keeping the Ramadan fast. His intense devotions are marked with visions and hallucinations.

When Muhammad emerges from these spells, he is convinced that Satan, the evil one, is the source of the strange visions. Often his limbs tremble while his face moves convulsively while breaking out in sweat. At times he falls in a coma and into deep sleep. During the night he produces a humming sound. He often asks his wife to cover him with warm clothes in order to reduce his fear. In this state of delirium he sees images accompanied by devastating dreams. Khadijah treats her husband calmly with much love and affection. She always approaches her cousin, Waraqa, for help during these stressful times.[26]

Muhammad's Literacy

During the forty-four years when Muhammad and Waraqa are closely involved with each other, the book that the priest is translating from Hebrew into Arabic is faithfully studied. Muhammad is fascinated, not only by the message of this Gospel of the Hebrews, but also by the Qiss' labors in the translation of the text into an Arabic book. The Qur'an gives numerous indications that the new translation task assumed by Waraqa opens up Muhammad to the divine words. For all of this to take place, it is necessary first to dispel the common misconception that Muhammad was illiterate (analphabet).

The firmly held belief that Muhammad lacked reading and writing skills goes against all evidences that he was literate. Part of the evidence for his reading abilities indicates that God does utilize natural abilities to announce his truth and his will. God entrusts his servant, Waraqa, to communicate with Muhammad by means of a literary device, the Gospel of the Hebrews. The Qur'anic expression "the illiterate prophet" means something other than what the majority of Muslims now hold onto regarding their prophet.

It is essential to distinguish here what Muhammad knew and what he did not know. What he knew was reading and writing already acquired in his childhood. The proofs for his literacy are clearly apparent in the Qur'an and elsewhere. Regarding what he did not know, but he would learn, is the science of the revealed book, meaning the science of divinities, spirituality and legislation. He will acquire this science, 'ilm, knowledge, by an individual who possesses the knowledge of the Book.

Muhammad learned the natural sciences in his childhood when he was under the protection of his grandfather and the tutelage of his uncle. Today, many of Muhammad's strongest devotees do not recognize that his reading skills developed as a youth. They deliberately stress that the revelations came as the direct intervention of God. These followers contend that because all the revelations are from God there is no need to find a human source in these revelations. However, I am submitting the following evidences to confirm that Muhammad acquired the natural science, literacy.

Firstly, the illiterate is, according to the Qur'an, the individual or group who do not own a holy book. The Jews, children of Isaac, son of Abraham, are People of the Book (*Ahl al-Kitab*), whereas the Arabs, children of Ishmael, son of Abraham, are the illiterates in pre-Islamic Arabia. The Qur'an makes this distinction. He invites the People of the Book and the illiterate Arabs to follow Islam: "Say to the People of the Book and to those who are unlearned: Do you submit yourselves?" (3:20). It expresses the desire of the illiterate to learn the Book (the holy scriptures): "There are among them illiterates who do not know the book, but mendacious tales" (2:78). Muhammad manifests his pride when God chooses him from among the non-Scriptural people. "God sent a messenger chosen among them" (7:63). The People of the Book knew well that this difference between them and the illiterate was an evident thing. "There is no call on us than to find a path for the illiterates" (3:75).

In this regard it is necessary to understand the Qur'anic understanding of Muhammad's illiteracy was a social standing rather than an individual situation. The following verses show that Muhammad believed that he came from an illiterate background. "People who follow the messenger, the illiterate prophet" (7:157) and "Believe in God and in his messenger, the illiterate prophet, who believes also in God" (7:158).

The illiterates are the Arabs, children of Ishmael, while the People of the Book are the Jews, children of Isaac and the Christians who had the Gospels. Consequently, Muhammad's illiteracy never means that he ignored reading and writing but rather he was one of the illiterate Arabs, children of Ishmael, who did not have a holy book.

Secondly, archangel Gabriel indicates evidence of Muhammad's literacy in the announcement when he addresses Muhammad in the opening verses of Sura 96.

> *"Read in the name of your Lord,*
> *Who created man out of a mere clot*
> *of congealed blood.*
> *Read! For your Lord is most bountiful,*
> *He who taught you the use of the pen*
> *and taught man which he did not know."* (1-6)

Research studies dealing with the Qur'an's own self-examination, the Compilers of the Sirahs of the messenger, Hadith and Sahih, all confirm that the above-mentioned Sura is the first one to appear in revelation. Many Muslim scholars agree that Gabriel, when he came to see Muhammad, held a book in his hand. If Muhammad was not able to read then this Qur'anic verse ordering the prophet to "Read" or "Recite" is something other than the common meaning for this important message opening up the revelation for Muhammad.

Muhammad should have acquired the natural sciences including his reading skills in the house of and under the protection of his uncle Abu Talib. One scholar describes the love of the latter for his nephew. He particularly showed Muhammad affection and honor. For several decades he devoted himself to him and protected him.[27]

The Compiler Ibn Sa'd comments about the close relations between Abu Talib and his nephew. "He loved him much more than his own children. When Muhammad went out, his uncle accompanied him. Abu Talib devoted his great love and reserved to Muhammad the best food." Further he adds, "Until his death, Abu Talib did not cease protecting, guiding and supporting Muhammad."[28]

This unusual arrangement, which the uncle extends toward his orphan nephew, almost automatically means that the adopted child would have benefited from the same education as provided to Ali, the birth-son of Abu Talib. Muhammad's cousin, Ali, became an author of a work called The Path of Eloquence (Nahj al-Balaghah). It does not appear likely that Abu Talib would have denied his beloved nephew from what his own son acquired. Abu Talib would never raise his nephew under his protection for satisfying only his minimum material needs, but would want to provide him all the education and good moral character as he did for his own son.

The Qur'an as Reading

"When you read the Qur'an, seek God's protection from Satan, the rejected one" (16:98).

"When you recite the Qur'an, we put an invisible veil between you and those who do not believe in the hereafter" (17:45).

"We have divided the Qur'an into portions, in order that you might recite it to men at intervals" (17:106.) "Read in your book! It is sufficient that you yourself make out an account" (17:14).

The Divine Science

The science Muhammad is ignorant of is that one which Waraqa takes care to transmit to his spiritual student. It is the science of the Holy Book that the monk is translating into Arabic in the presence of Muhammad. Muhammad studies this knowledge with Waraqa from the Hebrew Gospel. The new revelation accompanying the study of the Gospel will act as a legal document to help resolve disputes.[29] Through this knowledge, Muhammad and his followers will help Arabs charged with crimes. These persons are unable neither to be judged nor to be defended because they do not have a holy book. "Shall we then treat the Muslims like the people for sin? What is the matter with you? How judge you? Or have you a book through which you learn? That you shall have, through it whatever you choose" (68:35-38).

Those who have knowledge of the book accuse Muhammad for not bringing something new. But their accusations are turned against them. Indeed, his task is not to innovate but to study and teach the existing book. "Thus we explain the signs by various symbols, that they may make the matter clear to those who know" (6:105). Muhammad is the first among Arabs who will study and learn the book given by God in their language. "When our clear signs are rehearsed to them, they say: 'This is nothing but evident magic.' But we had not given them books which they could study, nor sent apostles to them before you as warners" (34:43-44).

Muhammad joins with others who study the book promising to tell only the truth. "Was not the covenant of the book taken from that they would not ascribe to God anything but the truth?" (7:169). Muhammad advises them to put into practice what they learn. "Be you worshippers of the Lord who is truly the Cherisher of all. For you have taught the book and you have studied it earnestly" (3:79). Those who disbelieve become like the Pharisees who are accused by Jesus because "They say contrary to what they practice" (Matthew 23:3).

For his part, Muhammad learns the lessons from the book. He will go on to expand upon these messages and to explain their meanings to his Arab friends. He now feels qualified to reply "to men who discuss about God without knowledge, without guide, and without an appropriate guidebook" (31:20; 22:8). The evidence indicates that Muhammad knows reading and possesses the divine science. His knowledge of this science does not reduce his role as a messenger, for God always chooses messengers and prophets to achieve the divine mission. God provides his servants all appropriate human means to bring the word to his people. However, when the Qur'an makes allusions to "the science which man does not know," it means the ignored knowledge of the revealed books.

Divine knowledge is neither intuition nor revelation. It comes from learning and acquisition from people "who read the book before" (10:94). To those who say, " We know well that they say 'a man instructs him.'" He answers, "The tongue of him they wickedly point to is notably foreign, while (the Qur'an) is pure and clear Arabic" (16:103).

Muhammad admits this charge and actually confirms it. "I do not tell you I own God's treasures and I know hidden things" (6:50; 7:188). Other arguments in the Qur'an testify to Muhammad's knowledge. Numerous witnesses are attributed in this framework to God, to angels and to the People of the Book: "Sufficient for a witness between me and you is God and those who have knowledge of the Book" (13:43). "That is this witness of God, his angels and those endued with knowledge" (3:18). "A witness from among the children of Israel testifies to its similarity with earlier scriptures" (46:10).

When Muhammad faces doubts of his own knowledge of God's revelation, he is instructed to ask the People of the Book for advice. "If you were in doubt about what has been sent to you from above, ask those who read the book before you" (10:94). This answer appears on two other occasions when there is further doubt. "Ask the men of Scriptures, if you do not know it" (16:43; 21:7).

The Qur'an is recalling what has been previously given. "Unto you we have sent down the message (the Qur'an) that you may explain clearly to men what is sent for them" (16:44). Among the people "having the knowledge of the book" and who give a witness of the Qur'an and the messenger, one will find Waraqa, a near relative to Muhammad and his wife, Khadijah.

Muhammad Succeeds Waraqa

Waraqa does not hide his intention regarding his pupil, Muhammad. The Compilers of Muhammad's Sirahs refrain from mentioning the special relationships that existed at the time of Waraqa's death. However, they cannot help but confirm Muhammad's prophetic ministry while in fact they are confirming that of Waraqa's. They maintain that they rely totally on the power of God, and do all to bind Muhammad to God without human intervention. By checking Waraqa's prophecies on Muhammad's future, one gets the impression that the biographers mention them to underline the priest's power and his basic role, while they intended to be speaking on behalf of Muhammad's prophecy.

Nothing is surprising in this affair. All is well prepared. Everything turns out well for Waraqa for various reasons. As a head and lord of Arabs, he benefits from a privileged status. He presides over the Nosrania community in Mecca. He has an abundant knowledge of scriptures. People revere him as they revere the other priests and hermits "who are not arrogant" (5:82). The poor who come to get advice, to find accommodation in their hermitages and to offer their prayers, frequent these. Some of these priests were able to foresee the future and to reveal mysteries.

Waraqa Ibn Nawfal holds several winning cards in his hands. His selection of Muhammad is most precipitous because he is the male Qaraysh family member who is closest to him and others of this clan. His plan undoubtedly was supported by Khadijah, Muhammad's wife, Abu Talib, his uncle and protector, Abu Bakr al-Siddiq, his intimate friend and future father-in-law. All abide by God's directives through Waraqa whose plan has been endorsed by other priests such as Bahira from Syria and 'Addass of Ninive.

Chapter III

Prophetic Announcements for Muhammad

The Compilers of the Sirahs of Muhammad present a number of events during the first fifteen years of his public ministry in Mecca. Many of these events will accompany messages as well as act as predictors of the coming revelations. I have reduced these predictors to six publicly acclaimed announcements.

First announcement: Prior to Muhammad's Marriage

One day, Muhammad accompanies a business caravan for Khadijah to Syria. During that trip, the faithful servant of Khadijah, Mayssarah, who was in that convoy, suddenly returns to his patron in Mecca. He tells Khadijah what he has seen and heard regarding a curious phenomenon that happened to the young Muhammad.[1] Instantly, Khadijah goes to inform her cousin, Waraqa, who does not manifest any astonishment. On the contrary, he shows an attitude worthy of somebody already informed of God's will. Otherwise, Waraqa would have explained to her what he knew in his heart. "If this is true, Muhammad will be the prophet of this nation. I knew there will be a prophet for this nation and his time is coming."[2]

The question arises, not about the truth of Muhammad's prophecy, but about that of the priest. From whom does he get this revelation? How has he known the will of God? Were the Christian monks and priests of that time able to predict the people's future? Why do Muhammad's devoted Compilers recognize Waraqa's predictions, without also recognizing one of God's servants who saw the divine purposes of the Arab messenger? In any case, Khadijah knows well how she should be aligned with the mission of her close cousin, Waraqa. She usually seeks his help, according to a Compiler who wrote: "Khadijah is behaving so in conformity with Waraqa's advice."[3]

Second announcement: At the Confrontation with Gabriel

Muhammad is age forty when he seeks solitude and withdrawal in a cave in Mount Hira' near Mecca, where he spends the usual month of Ramadan in fasting, praying and contemplation. At the end of that month, according to several Compilers, the archangel Gabriel appears to him and announces, "O Muhammad! You must know I am Gabriel and you are the apostle of God." He gives him a book to read. Frightened, Muhammad goes home immediately following the meeting with the archangel. He tells his wife what he has seen and heard. Khadijah, with her own keen awareness of God, announces, "Be reassured, courageous and patient. In the name of the One who has Khadijah's soul in his hands, I hope you will be the prophet of this nation." Immediately she hurries to her cousin, the Qiss Waraqa, and tells him what she heard from her husband.

Before she ends her report, Waraqa quietly announces, "Holy! Holy! In the name of Him who has my soul, you believed in me. The great law descending on Moses is coming also on him. He is the prophet of this nation. Tell him he must hold fast and resist."[4]

These testimonies on Muhammad's prophecy persist from heaven and earth, namely from Gabriel, Khadijah and Waraqa. The contents, the interpretations and the objectives are identical. The advice is for Muhammad to hold fast. Everywhere his future prophecy is announced to the Arab nation that was still living in the rough Jahiliyyan period. Muhammad comes from the same line like Moses and Jesus. He will bring a law for the illiterate Arab tribes, much like Moses and Jesus who brought a divine law to the People of the Book.

According to the new law, there will be no difference between Israel's children and the Arabs. The law is the same. Muhammad has only to claim that he is the messenger, the warner and the transmitter. Even here one has to question, not about Muhammad's prophecy, but about that of Khadijah who announces his prophecy. How was she able to know the divine will, to interpret a vision if she is not gifted with perceptions to unveil mysteries? Who informed her of this fact? God or her cousin Waraqa? God alone knows the answer!

Third announcement: At the Beginning of His Mission

Muhammad comes down from Mount Hara' at the end of Ramadan. He immediately returns to al-Ka'ba, circumventing it seven times according to the usual tradition. At that time, Waraqa also follows the same steps around the Meccan sanctuary. He asks the future prophet, "Dear cousin, tell me what you have seen and heard?" Muhammad relates all to him. With the calm of an obedient servant-priest, al-Qiss Waraqa, announces, 'In the name of him who has my soul, you are the prophet of this nation. The great law coming down on Moses is coming down also on you. If I am still alive on that day, I will contribute to God's victory'. He comes close to him and kisses him on the top of his head. Then, Muhammad goes home peacefully."[5]

It is this assurance that Muhammad is seeking. This confirmation from Waraqa is the same assurance that the Ebionite priest gives to his community. He succeeds in finding a successor to preside over the clan in Mecca. What is required of Muhammad now is to hold fast and to be assured. At that moment, al-Qiss is able to say, "I will contribute to God's victory." Hence the young man needs confirmation through the kiss on the top of his head. With this sign of approval, Muhammad announces his future mission that the Qur'an supports. "Their hearts find satisfaction in the remembrance of God" (13:28). "What God made is a message of hope for you and an encourager" (3:126).

With this familial protection, the One Supreme God, too, supports Muhammad and his followers. "God sent down his peace upon him. He strengthened him with mighty forces" (9:40). "God sent down his tranquility to his messenger and to the believers" (48:4; 9:26). The priest Waraqa gains a victory, which God grants him through this victory of his disciple.

Fourth announcement: The Time of the First Revelation

After this victory, Muhammad goes with his close friend, Abu Bakr, to see Waraqa. Abu Bakr asks for an explanation of the hallucinations and fainting spells but Muhammad refuses to give the reasons, the origins and the meanings for the experiences in the Khalwah cave. He expects answers from Waraqa in order to obtain some helpful guidance. "If I am left alone, I hear behind me a voice calling: 'Muhammad! Muhammad!' I take to flight." Waraqa tries to relieve him by offering counsel to quiet his fear. "Don't do anything if you hear again this voice! Hold fast and try to understand what will be said, then return to me."[6]

Meanwhile Muhammad's visions and hallucinations are increasing. He returns to his spiritual master to question Waraqa on the causes for his mental disturbances. The Qur'an lists a number of alternative sources for these provocative visions. Are they "a set of dreams" (21:5) generated by the evil one? Is it a kind of "madness" (7:184) or "a magic act" (6:7) empowered by a magician, or poetical inspiration by a great "poet" (36:69), or "a ribald priest or poet" (52:29,30); who is identifying these metaphysical experiences as God's treasures? Are the revelations coming down to him like revelations already delivered to the Old Testament's prophets?

Khadijah for her part continues her wifely support. She seeks solutions to relieve the fears of her husband. At times, she accompanies him to see Waraqa and on other occasions to see another monk, 'Addass of Ninive. One day she hurries to the latter to tell him what is happening to her husband. 'Addass questions, "Khadijah, is it possible that Satan has appeared to him? Take this talisman and give it to your husband. If he is a madman, the evil will run away. And if these things are coming from God, he will not have any trouble." Khadijah accepts the talisman and returns to her husband.[7]

Muhammad's most prominent biographer, Ibn Ishaq, reports that a liquid runs over Muhammad's eyes during these fainting spells that regularly occurred before revelations. Ibn Ishaq cites these incidents in an early hadith. "Muhammad's eyes turned misty with a liquid before the Qur'an has fallen on him... Following such revelations he suffered from the same physical reactions."[8] On these occasions, Khadijah offers, "I will send you somebody to wet your eyes." Ibn Ishaq comments, "I did not identify neither who wets his eyes nor the liquid with which they turned misty."[9]

Muhammad himself is terrified by these exotic and painful experiences. He often repeats, "I am afraid for myself."[10] "I am afraid to be a priest."[11] "I am afraid to be in a demoniac state."[12] In spite of all this suffering, Waraqa's hope for Muhammad's mission does not slacken and he often tells the future messenger of God to remain firm even through the times of great doubt.

Ask the People of the Book

"Ask the People of the Book, if you do not understand this (16:44; 21:7).

"They are those who receive God's guidance in the straight path. Follow their guidance" (6:90).

"There is among the people of Moses a large number of men who follow the truth as a guide and do justice" (7:159). "Among those we have created, there are people who follow the straight   p a t h , direct others with truth and dispense justice therein" (7:181).

"You will know who is on the straight way and who has received guidance" (20:135).

Fifth announcement: After the Mission's Beginning

Muhammad accepts Waraqa's advice from the beginning of the prophetic mission by preaching directly to the Meccans. He announces the Qur'an's verses that are now descending on him in a clear Arabic language. But he is not fully able to assume this mission because of his anxiety and distress.

While he is reciting, warning and preaching to the Meccan people, his body starts trembling, his face moves convulsively, filling Muhammad with apprehension. He immediately returns to his wife crying, "Zammilouni! Zammilouni!"-- "Cover me with warm clothing."[13] Khadijah covers him quickly d spelling the fears and the distress. Then he tells his wife what is happening to him. Khadijah's reaction is a surprise. She declares, "No! In the name of God, rejoice! God will never forsake you! You will touch the hearts! You will confirm what has been said! You will transmit all to others! You will do good for those deprived! You will provide hospitality to the needy! You will be replacing trials with truth."[14]

To confirm to her husband what she has said, she goes as usual with him to her cousin Waraqa, "Dear cousin! Listen to your nephew!" she entreats.

"Dear nephew! What did you see?" asks Waraqa.

When Muhammad finishes his report, the priest questions him and repeats earlier admonitions. "It is the same law transmitted to Moses." But this time, Waraqa adds, "Ah! If I could be young to live the mission's time!" To Khadijah, Waraqa declares, "Oh yes. Nobody came to see me with a man like this one with whom you are coming. Go home now."[15]

Sixth announcement: At the Beginning of the Peaceful Jihad (Struggle)

Ali, son of Abu Talib relates, "When Muhammad hears the appeal, 'Say: There is no divinity but God and Muhammad is his messenger.'" The prophet answers, "Labbayk (as you will)." Then Ali adds this doxology that becomes part of the first Sura. "Praise be God, Lord of the Worlds, the Compassionate, the Merciful, King of the day of Reckoning" (1:1-3). In hearing these words, Muhammad shows concern for what he hears. The priest replies, "It is announced to you! Announce it now! I bear witness that you are the man already announced by the son of Mary. You are on the way of Moses' law. You are a sent prophet. One day you will order the Jihad. If in that day I am still in life, I shall participate with you in this Jihad."[16]

Waraqa provides a significant start by his announcement. Muhammad realizes he must follow this Jihad's order to continue the struggle against any opponents. However, in the next moment, Waraqa becomes nearly deaf and blind. Muhammad reveals a sign of satisfaction, as he will not be alone in this Jihad against the troublesome hypocrites among his Qurayshi clan. He is relieved to see the aged Ebionite priest staying close to him. Waraqa cautions him to move slowly to reach a divine objective. It is advice underlined later in the Qur'an. "Be patient like courageous men among the apostles, do not be in a hurry" (46:35).

Directly after the passing of Waraqa, Muhammad depends upon the Qur'an's assurances that come with warnings about forgetting. "Perhaps you will forget to make known a part of what it is revealed to you and your heart will be in distress" (11:12). On the other hand, God will not forget his prophet without support. "Your Lord has never forgotten you or taken a strong aversion to you" (93:3). Muhammad should not forget what has been said to him in the book, "We shall give you to read. Do not forget" (6:89).

All situations providentially reveal that Muhammad has been encorporated into Waraqa's plan. Khadijah, the fortunate lady of Quraysh, is prepared to facilitate the plan for Muhammad's mission by providing money, notoriety, honor, beauty and love.

All has been arranged by Waraqa and executed by Khadijah in the best manner. This Arab woman establishes the link between Waraqa and Muhammad.   She listens to Muhammad to enccurage him, often scurrying to Waraqa to seek helpful guidance. Many times this citation if quoted, "Khadijah executed all in conformity with Waraqa's advice."[17]

Waraqa, Khadijah and Abu Talib played a preeminent role in Muhammad's life and mission. Following their deaths after 619, the loss of their intimate, emotional support was immense. With Waraqa's death, "revelation dried up."[18] With Khadijah's death, "trials increase in the messenger's life, for she was for him and for Islam an honest witness. He relies on her."[19] "She believed in him and in what was coming down from God. She was among the first people who believed in God, in his messenger. She consoled him when he came to see her."[20]

After the death of Abu Talib, "the Qurayshi clan does harm to God's messenger.   When he was alive, Abu Talib protected his nephew by standing with him to overcome the moves against him by his own clan."[21]

The priest Waraqa, whose death preceded Muhammad's wife and uncle, conceived the initiatives for Muhammad. Khadijah executed them and the uncle supported them. Being confident of this trio's guidance, Muhammad devoted himself completely to God's will. These three Quraysh relatives built the foundations of the mission that was carried out with great success by Muhammad. The truth is when the Lord chooses his prophets, he provides them appropriate circumstances granting the successes for their devoted efforts.

The Priest as the Prophet

What was the priest's intention?   What did he promote by his own announcements? -- Muhammad's prophecy or his own religious authority?

Later when Muhammad's Compilers begin to belittle the priest's intentions, they are distracted by the oral tradition that favors the study of law rather than the pursuit of history. These legalists receive little information on the priest's role in Muhammad's prophecy. These detractors never did question how religious authority (al-Qussussiyyah) was transmitted by the Nosrania sect to those following Islam.

However, since there was skepticism that Muhammad was not truly a prophet, the legalists looked for signs by tracing back to the first days of Adam. They continued to look for signs by claiming that rabbis, anchorites, priests, magicians, jinns, devils, animals, idols, trees, and stones, supported the prophet's messages. They insisted that his name is found in the Pentateuch and the Gospel. At the same time they ignored the legitimate al-Qiss Waraqa who was the first to declare Muhammad as a prophet.

This evidence shows that neither Waraqa nor Muhammad understood the prophecy in the framework of the Old Testament. It appears that the priest's intentions differed from Muhammad who ended up with something other than prophecy. Waraqa Ibn Nawfal's aim was to announce Muhammad as his own successor to become the head of the Nosrania community in Mecca.

Muhammad understood this task that was expected of him. He started to preach and warn people and to teach them what they did not know from the book. He showed them the direct way and the valid religion. He warns them about the conditions of the last judgment. He commanded them to do alms and acts of mercy. He read them texts extracted from the book. He knew well that his task was essentially in remembering for the people of the Torah and the People of the Gospel. "Warn! Thou art only a warner!" His book is a warning or a recalling of the Gospel of the Hebrews that was in Waraqa's hands. Muhammad was present for the transmission of this book into Arabic during their forty-four years together.

After the death of Waraqa, Muhammad has been invested with religious leadership. But he fears that God may forsake him or forget him, since "revelation has dried up" for nearly two or three years. It comes back after several modifications of the original message. The changes occur in conformity with Muhammad's personality and independence from his master the priest Waraqa. Later in Medina, Qur'anic revelations will build upon the earlier revelations in Mecca. "We have made it a Qur'an in Arabic that you may understand" (43:3).

The Priest Bahira recognized

A contemporary Sunnite dignitary known as a specialist in Islamic studies, Sheikh Sobhi al-Salih, recognizes only one meeting between Waraqa and Muhammad. He writes, "What can the prophet learn from two meetings, one with al-Qiss Waraqa and the other with al-Qiss Bahira, on metaphysics and history? Waraqa died a short time later, but Sobhi leaves out the end of the sentence, "and revelation dried up."[22] The Sheikh infers that "Muhammad met Waraqa at the end of his life. He found him an old man and blind. He was not able to do anything."[23]

A modern Egyptian, Muhammad Hussayn Haykal, author of an encyclopedia on Muhammad's life, expresses the same attitude toward Waraqa. He passes in silence over Waraqa's person and role. Among all meetings and declarations, Haykal mentions only incidental contacts.[24] What is the reason of this obvious omission? If it is the result of ignorance, it will be a serious violation of the facts.

Currently the Christian monk Bahira is almost universally praised while Waraqa largely ignored. What is the reason? It seems in this connection that dissimulations have altered the truth regarding Waraqa. In spite of his privileged position in the Meccan clan, his leadership of Nosrania Christians and his long physical and spiritual contact with Muhammad himself, this is all set aside. The Syrian monk Bahira had only limited contact with Qurayshi tradesmen in his hermitage in Basrah (locality situated in southern Syria near the frontiers with Jordan). Al-Qiss Bahira had only slight impact because all Muhammad's sojourns in this area were insufficient for him to learn and to benefit from any contact with this Christian hermit.

Historiographers and biographers have concentrated on the role of Bahira in Muhammad's life and succeeded in showing him in a favorable light detrimentally to Waraqa. This research is to help one focus on the far greater contribution that Waraqa offered than any possible role that Bahira could ever offer.

Chapter IV

The Gospel According to Waraqa

The significant Compilers, along with the Hadith collectors, including Muslim Ibn al-Hajjaj,[1] al-Bukhari[2] and al-Isfahani[3] are in agreement that the Ebionite priest Waraqa translated the Hebrew Gospel into Arabic. What is this Gospel and what are its teachings will be the subject of this current chapter.

The search for the sources of this gospel can be found in the records of the early Church Fathers. Their publications are impressive indicators regarding the first four centuries of recognizing this Hebrew Gospel. This little known apocryphal gospel eventually became embedded in the Arabic Qur'an making it an important link to "the preserved table" *(al-lawh al-mahfouz)* from which the Qur'an emanates.

Sources of Hebrew Gospel

The earliest church historian, Eusebius, (d. 340), quoting Hijsub, who lived in the beginning of the second century, records "that the latter reproduced the text of the Gospel according to the Hebrews, i.e. the Aramaic Gospel which was in Hebraic language."[4] Eusebius, the father of church history, certifies "this Gospel is the most credible for the Hebrews who believed in Jesus Christ."[5] In reference to the Ebionites, he writes, "They used only the Gospel called the Hebrews and did not show any interest in other Gospels." He adds, "They kept the Sabbath day and various Jewish traditions. They exhorted one another to put into practice the Pentateuch's precepts. They considered that man's salvation is not limited to only belief in Jesus Christ, but in performing also the law of Moses."[6] Other comments from Eusebius include, "Jesus Christ spoke about divisions from which human souls will suffer with their families according to quotations found in the Hebrew Gospel."[7]

Origen (d. 252) mentions this Gospel in several works. "The one who reads the Gospel according to the Hebrews will find the following verse: 'My mother, the Holy Ghost raised me with a hair from my head and took me to the big Mount Thabour.'"[8] Further he adds, "The young rich man, according to the Hebrew Gospel, scratched his head and did not accept Christ's offer. Jesus asks, 'How do you say that I have honored the prophets' laws and teachings, and you, you see your brothers, children of Abraham, and your house is bursting with wealth?'"[9]

Clement of Alexandria (d. 216) reads in that Gospel a cryptic sentence ascribed to Jesus Christ. "As it is written, in the Hebrew Gospel, the one who astonishes, owns, and the one who owns, has a rest."[10]

Epiphanius (d. 403) writes in his commentary on the Ebionists and their Hebrew Gospel, "They are only attached to the Gospel of Matthew and called it the Gospel according to the Hebrews. The Gospel of Matthew, which was at their disposal, is not perfect, but it has been altered and still is incomplete.[11] Epiphanius is quoting here the saying of St. Irenaeus, bishop of Lyon (d. 208) who said, "Ebionists only use the Gospel of Matthew, but they have not the true creed in God."[12]

St. Jerome mentions this Gospel in several writings, namely Commentaries on Isaiah,[13] on Ezekiel,[14] on Ephesians,[15] on Matthew,[16] and in his Dialogue against Pelagians. In the latter he writes, "The Nosrania use the Gospel according to the Hebrews, written in Aramaic... It is preserved in the Library of Cesarea."[17] And in his book, "The Eminent Men," he writes, "The Gospel according to the Hebrews, that recently has been translated into Greek and Latin and used by Origen, indicates that James would have sworn not to eat bread from the day in which he drank the cup of the Lord and until he saw him returning from the dead. The Lord tells him: 'Eat the bread on the table,' and adds, 'Eat your bread, because the Son of the Man has returned from the dead.'"[18]

Other testimonies are mentioned in an essay published by M. J. Lagrange in the Biblical Review. This twentieth century publication inquires about the Hebrew Gospel, its teachings and its assignment to the Ebionists. Lagrange notes that only a few strands of the texts remain from this Gospel mostly quoted in the writings of Church Fathers.[19]

In summary, this early Gospel was well known according to several Christian apologists, including each of the above that lived over a wide geographical area during the first centuries of the Christian church. Originally it was written in Aramaic-Hebrew script prior to its translation into Greek, Latin and Arabic. An Arabic version was mentioned from the second to the end of the fifth centuries with some traces of it until modern times.

While the Church Fathers spoke about its unorthodoxy, the Ebionists adopted it. At times it was called the Nazerine Gospel, or the Hebrew Gospel, or the Ebionists' Gospel, or the Gospel of the Twelve Apostles. It is a version of the Aramaic gospel of Matthew, which has been cited as one of the sources of the later Gospels. The Hebrew Gospel or the Gospel according to the Hebrews will play a significant role in the transfer of both heterodox and orthodox doctrines into Muslim beliefs and practices.

Sectarian, Arabic Scriptures

As a matter of course, the presence of Ebionists in Mecca and Hijaz contributed to the existence of the Hebrew Gospel in that area. Further credence of its widespread existence comes from many Qur'anic references, namely by its teachings regarding Jesus the Messiah, the Holy Spirit, charitable good works, the last judgment, and the final destination of human beings. Jawwad Ali summarizes the Ebionist doctrine:

"They believe in one God, Creator of the worlds. They deny the position of the Apostle Paul on Jesus Christ. They honor the holy Sabbath day and the Lord's day. The majority among them believes that Jesus Christ is a man like all men. He is distinguished by the prophecy like all prophets sent before him. Some groups of Ebionists deny the crucifixion of Jesus. Other dissidents claim that the one who has been crucified was not the Christ, but someone who appeared like Jesus. They refer to the Gospel of Matthew according to the Hebrews."[20]

The text of the Hebrew Gospel adopted and re-written by Waraqa in an Arabic version was not a fully accurate translation, according to the norms and expectations even in those early days. The method is "closer to exegesis and apologetics than to translation and transmission in a literal sense."[21] It is without doubt the method used for the older scriptures, as well as by Waraqa Ibn Nawfal in his translation of this Gospel into Arabic.

As for the Arabic version of the Hebrew Gospel, there are few present day vestiges. For all that it is worth, archaeologists could have looked for and probably discovered a remnant of this valuable version under the dark Meccan sands. Despite this loss to modern students, the only useful and meaningful trail which remains from Waraqa's lifetime is the Arabic Qur'an itself. It welcomes all to examine its pages and compare it to the previous scriptures and to what has reached us from the Ebionist sectarian doctrines.

Muhammad admits that a guide, God and a messenger, who informed him about the "faith and scripture," revealed to him the right way. "You did not know what was the Book or the faith... You also, you will be guided towards the straight path" (42:52). He would never learn the Book's content without the aid of a master who had taught him what he did not know. "God has sent down to you the Book and wisdom, and taught you what you did not know before" (4:113). The day when he doubts what he knew, he would be advised to consult the people having the knowledge of the Book. "If you are in doubt... ask who read the Holy Books before you" (10:94).

The truth of Muhammad's book issues from the truth from a prior book. This is the knowledge that will reappear in the Qur'an much like a commentary on the previous scriptures. Again, a study of the Qur'an will establish it as the foremost witness to the earlier scripture available today.

The Arabic transmission of the Hebrew Gospel

The word "Qur'an" linguistically refers to either a lecture or commentary. This expression is a derivative substantive of the Aramaic triliteral verb. Its third letter is a weak consonant: Qro, neqro, qiryono. It could mean lecture (Qira'ah) or recitation (tilawah) of a written or printed text. The word Qur'an is used fifty-eight times with the definite article al- and twelve times without the definite article al. Also, the

Arabic uses an indefinite form to indicate that the Qur'an, in its Arabic translation, is revealed as it was in its original language as in this rhetorical question. "Is it in a foreign or in Arabic language? Tell them: It is a guide and a remedy for those who believe" (41:44). However, it has been made available in Arabic so that the Arabic speaking people may be able to understand it. "We sent it down in Arabic language, so that you can understand it" (12:2). "We sent it in Arabic language, so that you can understand it. The original, the mother of the book (*Umm al-Kitab*) is by us" (43:3,4).

The Arabic listeners will be aware of its details (its translation). "A book whereof the verses are explained in detail; a Qur'an in Arabic for people who understand" (41:3). They should learn its stories and tales. "We do relate unto you the most beautiful of stories revealed to you in this Qur'an" (12:3). The readers and the hearers will be free to determine any deviations and failings. "It is a Qur'an in Arabic without any crookedness therein, in order that they may guard against evil" (39:28). It is in Arabic so that Muhammad would be able to read it without depending upon others. "It will be said to him: Read in your Book, sufficient is your soul this day to make out an account against you" (17:14). It is in Arabic to allow the messenger, Muhammad, to announce its revelation in Mecca and in nearby localities.

"We have revealed you the book in Arabic so that you can warn the mother of villages (*Umm al-qurah*, i.e. Mecca) and the people living in its surroundings" (42:7). If the Arabs receive the book in a foreign language, they would not be able to understand its messages. They want a translation in their own language. "Had we sent this as a Qur'an in a foreign language, they would have said: Oh! If at least the verses of this book were clear and explained in detail?" (41:44). On the contrary, if foreign people have received it in Arabic, they would not be able also to believe in it. "If we have revealed it to any of the non-Arabs, they would not have believed in it" (26:198-201).

The Qur'an as a commentary of a foreign book

"Elaborated" (*Mufassal*) has, according to the Qur'an, two meanings: First, mufassal has the idea of Arabisized (*Muarrab*), translated from another language into Arabic, so that the audience and the readers could understand its content and behave in conformity with its precepts.

Muhammad agrees with the Meccans' claim to have the book for Arabic readers. "Had we sent this as a Qur'an in a language other than Arabic, they would have said: why are not its verses explained in detail (*fusilat*)?" (41:44). It is even confirmed that the foreign book transmitted into Arabic by a wise expert (*Khabir hakim*) who is gifted to translate verses of the foreign book into a clear Arabic language. "A book whereof the verses are explained in order to build a Qur'an in Arabic for people who understand" (41:3; 11:1).

Secondly, the term *mufassal*, meaning in detail or elaborated, also gives a clue to the organization of the book's verses into chapters and the translation of previous holy books in pursuance of facts, events and circumstances. This is done to enable the listeners to easily remember and learn the Qur'an. Muhammad often states his desire to use repetition as a way of learning the Qur'an. "We explain in detail the verses for people who understand" (7:32; 9:11). "He who had sent unto you the book explained in detail" (6:114). "For we had certainly sent unto them a book based on knowledge which we explained in detail" (7:52). "We have detailed the signs for those who receive admonition" (6:126). "We have already explained all things in detail" (17:12).

These verses and the following indicate that the Arabic Qur'an "has disposed" (tassarafa) of the Hebrew words and texts in order to provide the Arabic words and texts for the new believers.

"We have explained things in various ways in this Qur'an, in order that they may receive admonition" (17:41). "We have put it at their disposal (amongst them) in order that they may remember" (25:50). "We have explained to the people in this Qur'an every kind of parable" (17:89). "We have sent this down - an Arabic Qur'an - and explained therein in details some of the teachings" (20:113; 6:65).

The Commentary on previous books

The Qur'an expands, elaborates and details the teachings of the foreign book by taking into account the situation in Arabia at the beginning of the seventh century. "See how we explain the signs by various symbols" (6:46). This certifies (authenticates, *saddaqa*) the existence of an original book. Although the transmission's process has brought modification, its teaching continues to confirm that of the original book.

Muhammad often repeats this assertion to show the people the authenticity of what has been transmitted from "the book being in his hands." He makes every attempt to confirm that the Qur'an is really an authentication (tassadiq) of the Hebrew book (3:3). Other verses make similar claims, "The book confirms it in the Arabic tongue" (46:12). "This is a book which we have sent down, bringing blessings and confirming the revelations which came before it" (6:92). "It is He who sent down to you in truth the book confirming what went before it" (3:3). "He brings down the revelation to your heart, by God's will, a confirmation of what was at your disposal before" (2:91). "What we have revealed to you of the book is the truth confirming what was available before it" (35:31). "It is confirming what was at my disposal from the Pentateuch" (3:50; 46:30).

Non-Muslims, namely *Ahl al-Kitab* (the People of the Book or the Biblical Family), together have heard all these evidences. "When there comes to them a book from God, confirming what is with them" (2:84). "O ye people of the Book! Believe in what we have revealed, confirming what was already at your disposal" (4:47). "They reject all besides, even if it be truth confirming what is at their disposal" (2:91).

Muhammad has within his grasp at least part of the Pentateuch and the Gospel. He expanded on the original Hebrew Gospel for his Arabic listeners. He uses these previous scriptures to facilitate the learning and the memory skills of the Arabs. This Arabic book of Muhammad affirms that it "is not a tale invented, but a confirmation of the Scriptures revealed before it" (12:111).

The Qur'an, a Facilitated Reading

"We have indeed made the Qur'an easy... to understand and remember" (54:17,22,40).

"Verily, we have made (this Qur'an) easy, in your tongue, in order that they may give heed" (44:58).

"So we have made (the Qur'an) easy in your own language, that with it you may give glad tidings to the righteous and warnings to people given to contention"   (19:97).

"Read, therefore, of the Qur'an, as much as may be easy for you" (73:20).

Those who have the original book know when they are hearing the Qur'an they recognize that this book is coming from God. So they bow their heads to the ground and kneel. "Those who were given knowledge beforehand, when it is recited to them, fall down on their faces in humble prostration" (17:107). The worthiness of the Arabic commentary on the foreign book, lies in its easy presentation in a clear Arabic language. Arabs are able to understand and to learn it easily by heart. The Lord has sent as a messenger somebody who knows the language of this people, so that the truth can be clearly presented. "We sent not an apostle other than one who speaks the language of his own people, in order to make clear to them" (14:4).

Reminder of previous books

According to the Qur'an, *tazkirah* carries the idea of two reminders. First, it is a summary of stories regarding former prophets, their events, teachings and parables. Second, it is a reminder of what has been announced as part of the official Scriptures of the Pentateuch and the Gospel. In the first case, Muhammad is not charged in transmitting to "those who already believe in God" among Arabs and who hear his message. Nor does he deal with their traditions, their creeds and their ethical standards. He confirms this evidence several times. "This (the Qur'an) is an admonition" (38:1). "For it is indeed a message of instruction" (80:11). "But verily is a message for God-fearing" (69:48).

As for those who receive the knowledge and hold it, they do not need any reminders or a warning. They know the book as an integral part of their book with the verses "firmly established and including precepts (*muhkamat*) and verses which are allegorical (*mutashabihat*)" (3:7). The Qur'an is a sufficient reminder for Arabs to have full guidance. "Verily this is an admonition: therefore, to lead him on a straight path to his Lord" (73:19).

Considering the simplicity and facilitation of the book's teachings and legends, Muhammad learned them without any difficulty: "We have not sent down the Qur'an to you to be an occasion for your distress, but only as an admonition to those who fear God" (20:2). One can gather from these references that the Qur'an is an easy digest, as well as a competent summary of the Pentateuch and the Gospel. This digest form is for the Arabs and not for others among the people of the Book.

The Qur'an recognizes this indulgence toward the Arabs. "That is a concession and a mercy from your Lord" (2:178).

This indulgence has specific ends: "God wishes to lighten your difficulties" (4:28); "God has lightened your task, for he knew that there is a weak spot in you" (8:66). After all, unobtainable knowledge only leads to despair and weariness that demands that divine message be simplified. "Only a little knowledge is communicated to you" (17:85). However, there is even in this digest form sufficient knowledge to lead to truth that is often presented as 'warnings.' Those who avoid these warnings will not be excused. "Why do they turn away from admonition" (74:49)?

In the second idea for reminders, tazkirah calls attention to the warnings and the admonitions of all the former messages. Muhammad's role consists in reminding the people of God's prophets and their teachings. "Remind! Warn! You are no other than a warner" (88:21).

Muhammad Recalling the former Prophets

"Remember, in the book, Abraham" (19:41). "Remember, in the book, Moses" (19:51).

"Remember, in the book, Ishmael" (19:54). "Remember, in the book, Idris" (19:56). "Commemorate our servant Job" (38:41). "Commemorate Ishmael, Elisha, Zhul-Kifl and all the righteous" (38:48). "Commemorate our powerful men: Abraham, Isaac and Jacob" (38:45). "Commemorate our brother 'Ad" (46:21).

"Remember in the book, Mary" (19:16).

Waraqa's reminders to Muhammad

The Qur'an is simultaneously a reminder of the previous books that includes admonitions and warnings from the writing and the non-writing prophets. Both meanings of "reminder" (tazkirah) indicate that the present Arabic book, the Qur'an, is extracted from a former book. More will be said concerning Waraqa's involvement with both of these books. For now, it is important to see how Waraqa's non-Arabic sources were translated after elaborations into Arabic and then passed to Muhammad during the forty-four years they mutually lived in Mecca.

Much of this discussion so far relates to the fact that Muhammad did not know a foreign language and his own language, Arabic, was not a language that had its own Scripture. Further the Qur'an raises the question of whether Muhammad could read or write in Arabic. If he could not read, it would mean that someone other than Muhammad would give details, elaborate (fassala) the Hebrew gospel. Who could have explained (bayyana) its teachings, or who would have facilitated (yassara) it in a clear Arabic language?

All that Muhammad intended to do was to proclaim the book as an apostle and an announcer. This declaration is often repeated in the Qur'an. "Verily, we have sent you in truth as a bearer of glad tidings and a warner" (11:25).

Muhammad grasps this task perfectly and confirms it by saying, "I am only a man entrusted to announce and to warn" (7:188). What is often ascribed to Muhammad must be ascribed to Waraqa, who has faithfully dispensed (sarrafa) the book's teachings and facilitated (yassara) it in a clear Arabic language. He has digested the content of the book and the wisdom, so that the Arab Nosrania community of Mecca will become believers much like the Jews who earlier converted to Christianity. The worthiness of this great man, Waraqa, lies in his competence in choosing Muhammad as a student of great personal gifts of leadership, intelligence and wisdom.

Chapter V

The Unity of the Message

We know well that there were several versions of the Pentateuch and the Gospels with an ample supply of commentaries for both of these sacred texts. Some texts and commentaries have official approvals while others are decidedly apocryphal and spurious. The Qur'an mentions the Gospel as if there were only one Gospel, which is mentioned twelve times with the definite article (al). Several sources highlight the fact that Waraqa possessed the gospel known as the Hebrew Gospel. In fact, it is erroneous to say that he only had access to the Hebrew Gospel and not to other books like the Pentateuch, or other Gospels, nor to the theological Nosrania teachings borrowed from the church's oral tradition.

Indeed, the Qur'an collects much information and teachings borrowed from several sources both sacred and non-sacred. What the Qur'an extracts from the previous Scriptures is done to prove that there is a single purpose linking all of the holy books together.

Revelation is a continuous process. Later prophets complete the mission of prior prophets. Books of the New Testament are grounded on those of the Old Testament. The believer finds his link with God when he discovers the unity of the divine message. The Arabic Qur'an expresses this position of unity in very definite and succinct terms.

Revelation's Unity

Muhammad was deeply aware of the revelation's continuity. He did not bring a new revelation from nothing. The revelation he brings - or which has come down on him - is an assurance that he possesses the same message brought by former prophets. "We have sent you inspiration, as we sent it to Noah and the Messengers after him; we sent inspiration to Ibraham, shmael, Isaac, Jacob and the tribes...

And to David, we gave the Psalms" (4:163). Over and over, the Qur'an emphasizes that Muhammad's Revelation is identical to that given to his predecessors: "Thus God, exalted in power and full of wisdom, has sent inspiration to you as he did to those before you" (42:3). "It has already been revealed to you, as it was to those before you" (39:65).

The Qur'an's References to Former Scriptures

"What we have revealed to you of the book, is the truth confirming what was revealed before you (35:31). "Recite what is revealed of the book to you" (29:46).

"We reveal unto you unseen things" (3:44; 12:102); "Such are some of stories of the Unseen, which we have revealed unto you" (11:49).

"These are what your Lord has revealed to you" (17:39).

However, if the revelation ascribed to Muhammad is identical to that ascribed to former prophets, then it should be apparent in the previous revelation. Likewise, Muhammad's scriptures proceed from a pre-existing book where most of the texts of the previous revelation were clearly revealed. There are several references to mystical aspects of the revelation as well. This is hinted at as the "preserved table" (*al-lawh al-mahfouz*) (85:22) or from the "hidden book" (*al-kitab al-maknun*) (56:78). Muhammad himself did not know the mysteries or the hidden things. "Tell them: I do not say that I own the treasures of God, that I know the mysteries or the hidden things" (6:50; 11:31); "No one other than God knows the mystery or the hidden things" (27:65).

On the other hand, God gives him the revelation from a mystery, that means from hidden things or the unseen (*al-ghayb*) world. This ostensible paradox is no problem for Muhammad who becomes the conduit through which the mystery or the hidden things are revealed.

Tanzil's Unity

Qur'anic revelation, or that which comes down (*tanzil*) suggests a former tanzil, or it is an explanation (*tibyan*) of what has been revealed before. Muhammad's mission is to show people the entirety of what has been coming down on former prophets. He draws upon and copies them. He refers to these prophets and borrows their stories, tales and parables in order to explain all to the Arabs. "We have sent down to you the book explaining all things" (16:89). "We have sent down unto you the Message that you may explain clearly to men what is sent for them" (16:44). "God wishes to make clear to you and to show you the ordinances of those before you" (4:26). "God took a covenant from the People of the Book to make it known and clear to men" (3:187).

The Qur'an explains throughout its pages that the former book also is a product of direct tanzil. He calls the scripture of the People of the Book (Ahl al-kitab) as a witness. Muhammad considers the Nosrania as if they have already been informed of the truthful content of their book. "To whom we have given the book, know that it has been sent down from your Lord in Truth" (6:114). "Those to whom knowledge has come, see that revelation sent down to you from your Lord - That is the truth" (34:6)

The people with Scriptures, the Jews and Christians, believe in the former book and some of these who form the sect, the Nosrania, will accept the Qur'an. "But those among them (the Nosrania) who are well-grounded in knowledge, and the believers (among Arabs) believe in what has been revealed before you (the Pentateuch and the Gospel)" (4:159). The Muslims are those who say, "We believe in God and the revelation that has come to us and that which came before us" (5:59). "Those who believe in the revelation sent to you and sent before your time" (2:4). Those who read previous revelation testify to the genuineness of the Arabic tanzil and can vouchsafe that the Scriptures are true. "If you are in doubt as what we have revealed unto you, then ask those who have been reading the Scriptures before you" (10:94).

People Unity

The Nosrania who were once Jewish at the beginning of Muhammad's ministry are cautioned not to become jealous on account of what has been sent to Muhammad. "Those to whom we have given the book rejoice at what has been revealed unto you" (13:36). Also, illiterate Arabs should not protest against the messenger because the messenger did give them a book written in their own language. In this regard, he cautions, "You should say: 'the book was sent down to two peoples before us, and for our part, we remained unacquainted with all that they learned by assiduous study'" (6:156).

Muhammad seriously understood his task. He did not leave anything in the former book without taking it into consideration. Animals and birds form communities that are akin to the unity that the book stresses. "We didn't neglect anything in the book, and they shall be gathered to their Lord in the end" (6:38). The messenger of God knew well the faith and the ethical system emerging from the Pentateuch, the Gospel and the Qur'an. "You have no ground to stand upon unless you stand fast by the Pentateuch, the Gospel and all the revelation that has come to you from your Lord" (5:68).

Law's Unity

Revelation's continuity is confirmed through the continuity of the law since Noah, Moses and Jesus, and all the prophets and tribes up to Muhammad. This sacred law (*Shari'a*) is eternal. "But no change will you find in God's way of dealing" (35:43). It is the same law conceived by Noah. "He established for you the same religion as that which he enjoined on Noah" (42:13). The apostles and the prophets have brought it. "This was our way with the apostles we sent before you" (17:77).

Muhammad's role consists in explaining to his people the law and traditions (Sunnah) of the first prophets and by helping in their understanding of the law. "God wishes to make clear to you and to show you the Sunnah, ordinances, of those before you" (4:26).

However, a discrepancy appears between the tradition of Muhammad and that of his predecessors. This discrepancy appears in the divine allowances, alleviation (al-khiffah) of the Muhammadan Shari'a. God so desires to allow for humankind's weakness and frailty. "God intends every facility for you. He does not want humans to face difficulties" (2:185). "God wishes to lighten your difficulties: for man was created weak (in flesh)" (4:28). The reason for these allowances is to establish Muhammad's message for a particular community. "To every people an apostle was sent" (10:47).

The messenger to the Arabs should not be like the Mosaic messenger. He should not legislate a law like the Jewish one. God has established an appropriate mission for each people. "God knows best where to carry out his mission" (6:124).

Believers' Unity

Arabic and Hebrew revelations are inseparable. The first explains the second and refers to it. The second is the witness for the first. Believers among Arabs must adhere to the former faith because it is the origin and the confirmation of the Arabic revelation.

The Qur'an speaks to believers among the Arabs. "Say: We believe in God and in what he has sent to us, to Abrahim, to Ishmael, to Jacob" (2:127; 3:84). "Say: We believe in this book revealed to us, as well as in what has been revealed to you. Our God and yours are One" (29:46).

The Truth of All Revelations

"Those to whom knowledge has come see that the revelation sent down to you from your Lord - That is the Truth" (34:6). "To whom we have given the Book, know that it has been sent down from your Lord in Truth" (6:114). "When they listen to the revelation received by the apostle, you will see their eyes overflowing with tears, for they recognize the Truth" (5:83). "Truth has arrived, and falsehood perished" (17:81).

"O People of the Book! You have no ground to stand upon unless you stand fast by the Pentateuch, the Gospel and all the revelation that has come to you from your Lord" (5:68).

"O my Lord! Let my entry be by the gate of truth and my exit by the gate of truth" (17:80).

The Qur'an describes the genuine faith of people by their acceptance of the whole revelation. "But those among them (the Nosrania) who are well-grounded in knowledge, and the believers (among Arabs) believe in what has been revealed before you (the Pentateuch and the Gospel)" (4:162). "We believe in God and the revelation that has come to us and that which came before us" (5:59).

The Arabic and the Hebrew revelations are necessary. The Arabs and the children of Israel must believe in the Pentateuch, the Gospel and the Qur'an. He who only believes in the Pentateuch will be one of those Jews named by the Qur'an who rejected Jesus as the Messiah and as a prophet (2:87).[1] He who only believes in the Gospel will be one of those Christians who, according to the Qur'an, "exaggerates" his religion (4:171; 5:77). He who solely believes in the Arabic Qur'an, will be one of those Muslims considered as followers of Mushaf 'Uthman (the revisionists of the Qur'an at the time of Caliph 'Uthman) and not of Muhammad. These so-called Muslims are only heeding the Qur'an's laws and teachings and ignore the previous scriptures.

"O believers! Believe in God, in his apostle, in the book that has come to you and in the Scriptures coming down before it" (4:136).

As far as he who believes in all and respects all laws, he will be included among good Muslims who claim: "We believe in God and the revelation that has come to us and that which came before us" (5:59). These truly know and believe "that there is no god except Him whom the Children of Israel believe in" (10:90).

Who taught Muhammad?

There is an expected continuity in Revelation or tanzil from God to his prophets that should always be the same. The Arabic Qur'an should be like that found in the Hebrew Book. All that deals with men and their destiny, their ultimate salvation, should not change from the beginning but will be continued throughout eternity. Let me pose some questions here that will provide a key to understanding this unity and Muhammad's role in it.

-      How did Muhammad learn the former revelation?
-      Did God intervene in the life of Muhammad to teach him what he did not know?
-      Did an angel or archangel instruct Muhammad?
-      Did Muhammad alone discover the former revelation?

Facing these questions, let us consider two possible alternatives now. (1) Muhammad discovered the former revelation alone. This means that he learned it in its original Hebrew and proceeded to translate it into another language, the Arabic. (2) Muhammad became familiar with the prior revelation by means of a wise expert (*khabir hakim*) who taught him what he didn't know.

The first hypothetical answer (1) may immediately be dismissed because it has never been said that Muhammad understood Aramaic or Hebrew. However, the second suggested answer is more probable because Muhammad constantly refers to "those who have the science (knowledge) of the Book" (The People of the Book). He interrogates them. He calls them to testify on behalf of his mission so that he can be satisfied with their witness. "Say: Enough for a witness between you and me is God, and such as have knowledge of the Book" (13:43).

Muhammad learns much from the prior revelations which Waraqa, the wise expert, shares with him. However, there is very little about this source from the compilations and other historical books. Neither are there any other references to an individual other than the priest Waraqa who taught Muhammad what he did not know.

Apostolic Gospel Teaching

After acquiring what he did not know, Muhammad starts teaching what he has learned. Teaching those who fear God among the Arabs was one of the main tasks in the messenger's life. This task is the same as that of former prophets and Jesus, the Messiah, as it is announced, according to the Qur'an, to the children of Israel. "O children of Israel! I am the apostle of God sent to you" (61:6). In the Gospel of Matthew, Jesus is called "the master" (23:8). He taught the Jews in the Temple "the Good News of the Kingdom" (Matthew 4:23). He sent his disciples to announce the Good News "to all nations" (Matthew 28:19).

The Apostle Paul told his disciple, Timothy, "to preach the Word of God urgently, at all times, whenever you get the chance, in season and out, when it is convenient and when it is not. Correct and rebuke your people when they need it, encourage them to do right, and all the time be feeding them patiently with God's Word" (II Timothy 4:12).

The pastor-servant, Waraqa, assumed his apostolic task as a teacher. Teaching is a gift associated with preaching, which was what Jesus, the apostles, and Paul did as servants of the Lord. The apostle Peter announces this in his homily in Cornelius' house. "He sent us to preach to the people the Good News" (Acts 10:42). The Apostle Paul identifies the task of a religious man in saying, "But how can they believe in him if they have never heard about him?" Paul adds, "Yet faith comes from listening to this Good News" (Romans 10:14,15,17). It is the indispensable calling for any apostle to be an announcer who teaches the people and guides them on the straight path.

Muhammad, Waraqa's successor as a head of the Meccan Nosrania church, has been sent to preach and teach the faith to his people. However, to understand the faith one should listen to the words of the one sent and entrusted to preach. First Waraqa and then Muhammad received the call to teach God's truth to the Arabs.

Both explain to the Meccans God's precepts, forgiveness of sins and provide an ethical guide to keep them in the straight path. The Arab preachers should assume this task because the people are turning away from God and are devoting themselves to wealth and procreation of sons.

When it comes time for Muhammad to announce the message he brings with him the book of wisdom. He recites for them the book's verses so that they hear and believe knowing that none can believe without first hearing. Muhammad identifies his apostleship as one to teach what has been ignored. "God did confer a great favor on the believers when he sent among them an apostle from among themselves, rehearsing unto them the signs of God, sanctifying them and instructing them in the scriptures and wisdom, before that they had been in manifest error" (3:164). This message is found several times in the Qur'an. "We have sent among you an apostle of your own who is rehearsing to you our signs and sanctifying you and instructing you in scriptures and wisdom and what you ignored" (2:151).

Muhammad as a Warner

"I am but a warner and a bringer of glad tidings" (7:188).

"I am sent to you to warn and bring glad tidings" (11:2).

"We only sent you to give glad tidings and a warner" (2:119).

"Do you wonder that there has come to you a message from your Lord, through a man of your own people, to warn you" (7:63,69).

"Is a matter of wonderment to men that we have sent our inspiration to a man from among themselves, that he should warn men" (10:2).

"So they wonder that a warner has come to them from among themselves" (38:4).

Muhammad understood that his book was God's reminder to exhort him to preach and to be a guide to the truth. "The Qur'an has been revealed to me that I may warn you" (6:19). This is a book which we have sent down, bringing blessings and confirming what came before it, that you may warn the mother of villages (Mecca and surrounding areas)" (6:92). A book revealed unto you, so let your heart be oppressed no more by any difficulty on that account, that with it you might warn" (7:2). "This is a message for men, let them take warning there from (14:52). "This book confirms in the Arabic tongue to admonish the unjust" (46:ˉ2).

The Qur'an is no less than a book to be "an explanation of all things, a direction, a mercy an announcement for Muslims" (16:89). "It is a matter of wonderment to men that we have sent our inspiration to a man from among themselves" (10:2). If this message is too difficult for his friends and enemies among the Meccans, they have to request the witness of those having the knowledge of the book. "Ask the family of scriptures (Ahl al-Zikr), if you do not know it (16:43; 21:7). They can receive confirmation from the book people. "You will learn by this people having the straight path and who are converted" (20:135), that the Qur'an is coming down from God confirming the truth (3:7).

How often Muhammad called upon God to be a faithful proclaimer. "Grant me honorable mention of the tongue of truth among the latest generations" (26:84). In his hometown, Mecca, Muhammad was esteemed to be a man of faithfulness. He was called by the name al-'Amin, the faithful one.

It remains a major problem to recognize that behind Muhammad was a person who instructed him. Likewise it is a problem for the Muslim community to recognize behind the Qur'an another book to which it refers. Even as the priest of the Mecca Ebionite church is behind the prophet and blew on his ears the message from God, there looms a former book that is the source of much of the teachings and narratives of the Qur'an itself.

However, if the work of al-Qiss Waraqa becomes apparent and does not provoke any further problems, the recognition of the now lost Hebrew Gospel could become apparent as it is firmly embedded in the Qur'an. The Qur'an in its present 'Uthmani revision will provoke significant problems.

When one takes into consideration modern researches of the Qur'an, namely those like Professors Theodor Noldeke and Richard Bell who studied the arrangement of verses of the Suras and attempted to classify them in a systematic order, one will discover a very helpful fact.[2] The lesson to be learned is that the Meccan revelations are closely aligned with the Hebrew Gospel that was translated into Arabic by Waraqa. This is in contrast to the Medanese Qur'anic passages that often are violently disassociated from both the Jews and the Christians.

From the Meccan revelations we can deduce that the book used by Waraqa and his Nosrania congregation became the "Gospel of the Arabs." This fits into the revelation that sees, "each people will be called before his book," (45:28) and "each village will have its book" (15:4). Through the dedication of Waraqa, the Arabs now have their book.

Chapter VI

Islam before Islam-Nosrania
Sectarianism in Islam

This chapter will show that Nosrania faith did not become the exclusive apologia of sectarian priests and itinerant preachers like Waraqa who announced the Good News in Mecca and the Hijaz.

According to the historian al-Ya'qubi (d. 284),[1] a sizable number of Qurayshi tribe belonged to this Christian sect. These followers of the Nazarene Jesus, the Messiah, appear in the Ka'ba, a finding established by al-Azraki in his work "Excavations in Makka."[2] Waraqa, a Qiss (cult monk or priest), manages a section of the Meccan shrine's spiritual and material affairs. This religion was based upon a revealed book, namely "the Gospel according to the Hebrews." Several of the Compilers dealing with that historical period testify to the existence of a Nazarene affiliation within Muhammad's family. His grandfather, his parents, his uncles and his near relatives were adherents of Nosrania teachings. Itinerant priests, "adorators" of God, would have a profound influence on the young Muhammad and his subsequent ministry.

'Abd al-Muttalib as a Nosrania Follower

'Abd al-Muttalib, grandfather of Muhammad, "is considered among those who rejected the idols' culture in Jahiliyyah time."[3] A contemporary reports that 'Abd al-Muttalib "belonged to Abraham's cult, suggesting that he was not an idolatrous person."[4] Abraham's religion is "the orthodox one," which submits to monotheism thus condemning polytheism. According to the Qur'an, the worship of one God is "the constant religion" (9:33) or "the standard for religion" (12:40; 30:30). Several indicators testify that 'Abd al-Muttalib was Hanifite and monotheist, i.e. "adorator of God,"[5] a quality assumed by other Christians and Nosrania in Arab-speaking areas. He is not part of the greater Meccan population who combined worshipping the God alongside of idols.

'Abd al-Muttalib's life, along with his strong character qualities, his teachings and the counsel he gave to his children are the strongest indicators that he believed in an ethical faith based upon the idea of one God.

According to Ibn Hisham, 'Abd al-Muttalib was "one of the most charitable and most wise men of Quraysh." He accepts Muhammad's announcements about his call to be a prophet. He forbids alcohol for himself. He is among the first people who ventures to the cave in Mount Hara' to meditate and perform some ascetic practices. He enters the cave yearly at the beginning of the month of Ramadan. He extends himself by acts of charity to help feed the poor. When 'Abd al-Muttalib withdrew from society, he would pray and contemplate on God's goodness. He often shares his meals with birds and wild animals. For that reason, he was called "the feeder of birds" or simply, "the munificent."[6]

Another source extols the virtues of 'Abd al-Muttalib's devotion to monotheism, his exhortation to his children to practice generous acts, his visits to Mount Hara' and his compassion towards the poor, including his sharing food with birds and wild animals. This resource reports that he had a more legalistic side that agreed with the sentence for a thief, which was the cutting off of a thief's hand. Likewise, alcohol, adultery and incest were condemned. He never moved about his home unclothed. He often used the phrase: "In the name of God, there is behind this habitation another one where the benefactor will be rewarded and the malefactor sanctioned."[7]

'Abd al-Muttalib's rejection of any idolatrous tendencies specifically discloses his understanding of both Judaism and Nosrania practices. Both of these monotheistic faiths left their traces in Mecca and the surrounding Hijaz regions. The fact that his biographers underline 'Abd al-Muttalib's compassion toward animals and birds and his generosity toward the poor and the destitute, allows us to learn much more about the Nosrania sect of Ebionists rather than formal contacts with any Jews in the area around Mecca.

The Faith of Muhammad's Parents

Muhammad's grandfather's strict devotions to Nosrania Ebionism may also be seen by his frequent company with rabbis and priests. Certain authors often mention 'Abd al-Muttalib's meetings and discussions with monotheists who frequent this central Arabia area. Al-Siuti tells in this regard, "One day 'Abd al-Muttalib was at home in serious discussion with a bishop."[8] Al-'Abbas adds, "'Abd al-Muttalib reports that he has been in Yemen and stood by a rabbi who read the Psalms."[9] Ibn al-Jawzi notes, "Muhammad, who was seven years old, was suffering from a case of serious conjunctivitis. His grandfather conducted him to 'Ukaz to consult a priest who nursed ocular illnesses."[10] The Halabiyya biography reports, "'Abd al-Muttalib often left his home and went to 'Isa, a priest from Syria, to whom God granted a large knowledge and who never left his hermitage."[11]

The next question arises, "Were the parents of the future prophet for all Islam followers of the faith in the oneness of God like the godly 'Abd al-Muttalib?"

Very few concrete facts are known about Muhammad's parents, Abdallah and Aminah. They both died when their son was a young child and apparently had little influence in his education. They did not leave him the prescribed five she-camels, but an Ethiopian governess, Baraka, as part of a meager inheritance. Baraka, known by the nickname 'Umm 'Ayman (or 'Ayman's mother) was a Nosrania believer. She cared for the child and taught him good behavior. Muhammad responds with love and respect toward this servant. He often said to her, "You are my second mother."[12] On another occasion he is reported to have said, "He who likes to get married to a woman of paradise, he should choose 'Umm 'Ayman."[13]

That Muhammad's parents were of good standing and followed the straight path is widely recognized among the Compilers. Al-Fakhr al-Razi (d.1209) states, "Muhammad's parents were al-Hanifiyya, the religion of Abraham, like Zayd ibn 'Amran ibn Nufayl and his clan." However, this respected Arab source adds, "Polytheists were disgraceful. Any one of his ancestors could be among them."[14]

Eminent scholars such as al-Sannussi and Telemessani confirm al-Razi's sayings. They write, "His parents did not know polytheism. Both were Muslims. Muhammad's coming is from aristocratic beginnings of a pure womb. This can only be possible by faith in God. What some Compilers translated is indecent and immodest."[15] Jalal al-Siuti agrees with al-Razi by pointing to other indications that are found in letters on this subject of the purity of Muhammad's birth lines.[16]

Later, biographers surmised that "his parents were believers observing the laws of their prophets. Among them, nobody was impious or disqualified as an unbeliever."[17] It is clear that Muhammad's parents were "Muslims before Islam."

Abu Talib follows his father

At the death of his pious grandfather, 'Abd al-Muttalib, Muhammad is eight years old. His uncle Abu Talib takes charge of the boy's education and introduction to the Hashemite wing of the family that would include the clan's religious legacy. "Abu Talib assumes his duties regarding his nephew. He treats Muhammad as his son through respect and honor. He looks after him during forty years while gaining both friends and enemies because of his beloved nephew."[18]

When one weighs all the reports on Abu Talib, it is noteworthy that his virtues are much more part of the straight path associated with the monotheistic Ebionites rather than polytheistic qualities of his clan. Like his father, he looks after the poor and the destitute, though his family lives in humble circumstances. His last will and testament left to his children reveals the gentle qualities of his Ebionism. On his deathbed he urges them, "Answer to those who invite you and give to those who beg from you. Here lies the greatness of life and death."[19] He was distinguished through his kindnesses.

Ibn Sa'd reports, "Abu Talib went once to Damascus where he met a monk who would tell him, 'There is a good man among you.'" Abu Talib replies, 'Among us there is one who welcomes the foreigners, liberates prisoners and does acts of charity.'"[20] A significant word pronounced by Abu Talib helps establish his spiritual relationship to his own father. "I belong to 'Abd al-Muttalib's cult at the time of his death."[21] Others say, "that he was like his father."[22] In other words, Muhammad's uncle, Abu Talib, arises from the same spiritual background as his illustrious father. He rejected idolatry. He looked out for the poor. He practiced the usual devotions. He fasted the month of Ramadan. He belonged to the true religion, which could only mean al-Hanifiyyah, the monotheistic religion of Abraham among the polytheists from Quraysh.

General religious conditions in Mecca

The general religious environment in which Muhammad lived was neither polytheist nor atheist as certain groups maintain. In spite of accounts given in the Sirahs of the various Compilers' documents, the city of Mecca was not oblivious to the concept of a supreme God. The Meccans, although tending toward polytheistic practices in their ordinary life, never denied the divine unity centered in one God.

Mecca polytheism, as presented in the Qur'an, follows a pattern that avoids any association of other divinities with God. Yet there existed lower levels of devotion, of intercession and of rituals. A mediator of this polytheism may be an angel (37:150), a jinn (6:100), an idol (10:18), a prophet (3:80), or a natural power, like the sun, the moon, trees or stones (27:22). While the Arabs of Mecca never adored a human being as God, they considered the supernatural mediators able to intercede for them whenever they approached God.

The Qur'an does not blame the inhabitants of Mecca for their ignorance of God, but they are accused of falsely representing God through icons and idols. These images distort their own knowledge and their faith in God. Although they recognize God, they are creating other, lesser divinities. "Most of them believe not in God without associating (others as partners) with him (12:106). Arabs swear in the name of Allah that they do not belong to this group. "By Allah! Our Lord! We have not been made associates with God" (6:23).

Muhammad himself recognized this curious practice of his people. God is the Creator of heaven and earth which introduces a Qur'anic liturgical pattern. "If indeed you ask them: Who has created the heavens and the earth and subjected the sun and the moon (to his law), they will certainly reply, 'God'" (39:38). He adds several rhetorical questions, "Even if you send down from the sky and give life to the earth after death, they will certainly reply: 'God'" (43:87). The Qur'an asks, "Who manages the world? Who animates the earth? Who does well and does harm? They will say: 'God.' Say: Who is the Lord of the seven heavens and of the supreme throne? They will reply: 'God'" (23:86,87).

Further the liturgy taunts the Qurayshi tribesmen, "Who is it in whose hands holds the governance of all things? They will reply: God" (23:88). "Who brings out the living from the dead and the dead from the living, and who rules and regulates all affairs? They will soon say: 'God'" (10:31). "When they do what is shameful, they say: 'We found our fathers doing so and God commanded us thus'" (7:28). This paganism of the Arabs became a flat denial of their own conceptions of God's unity.

The Meccans might recognize God as the sole Creator, but they found God through the medium of images, through the intercession of angels and holy men, through symbols, statues and icons. Even the spiritual experiences of Muhammad would not be too different a faith than his family and his neighbors. However, Waraqa Ibn Nawfal provides company for Muhammad when the latter turns to the Ebionite priest for answers to difficulties that arose in the contradictory religious environment of the seventh century Meccans. These two bear witness of the monotheism of Nosrania. Further evidence of friendship and reverence expressed by Muhammad towards this Christian sect is also embedded in the Qur'an.

Islam the Perfect Religion
"The religion before God is Islam (submission)" (3:19). "If anyone desires a religion other than Islam, it will never be accepted of him" (3:85). "God will open by means of Islam the hearts of whom he will guide" (6:125). "He receives the guidance of his Lord" (39:22). "I have completed my favor upon you and have chosen for you Islam as your religion" (5:3). "Count not your Islam as a favor upon me. God would confer a favor upon you" (49:17).

Islam is the religion of Oneness of God. He will not admit any other religion than that which Muhammad announces to the Arabs. Some pertinent interrogations are unavoidable: Is Islam a new religion and Muhammad its first forerunner, or did it exist before him? Is there a divergence between the Nosrania teachings, which Muhammad learned from Waraqa, and Islam's teachings as found in the Qur'an?

Has Islam been created out of nothing or is it a new Arab form of prevailing Nosrania beliefs? Only the Qur'an is able to give real answers to these questions. Other answers outside this source are suspicious.

The Qur'an witness to true Islam

The Qur'an testifies that Islam existed among the children of Israel in pre-Arab empire times and that there were Arab Muslims before Muhammad and the revelation of Qur'an. All Muslims, according to this holy book, are those who do not make any difference between prophets, who follow both the Torah and the Gospel and who abide by the faith of Abraham. This faith of submission to one God has prevailed before the People of the Book and the Children of Israel were united -- not dispersed into sects, groups and parties. Abraham was Muslim before Judaism, Christianity and Islam. "Abraham was neither Jew nor Christian, he was true in faith" (3:67).

Together, Abraham and his son, Ishmael, pray and announce their submission to Islam. "Our Lord! Accept [our prayer]! Thou are he who hears and sees all things. Our Lord! Let us [both] be among Muslims" (2:127,128). The Hebrew Patriarch, Jacob, before his death, recommends to his sons: "O my children! God has chosen for you the religion; do not die other than Muslims [submitted to God]" (2:132). The sons of Jacob obey the urgings of their father when they testify, "We worship your God, God of your fathers: Abraham, Ishmael and Isaac, the one God, and we are Muslims" (2: 133).

The Qur'an also commands the prophet Noah to be of those who are Muslims. "My retribution depends alone from God and I received the order to be one of those who are Muslims" (10:72). Moses also recommends to his people: "If you believe in God, trust him if you are Muslims" (10:84).

The Pharaoh who tried to seek repentance on one occasion reportedly said, "There is no God except him whom the children of Israel believe in. I am among those who are Muslims" (10:90). Solomon, the wise, speaks to the queen of Sheba, "The science [knowledge] has come already to us and we were Muslims" (27:42).

Even the twelve disciples asked 'Isa [Jesus] to testify that they are Muslims (3:52); and in the same context, God said, "I have revealed to the Apostles to believe in me and in my Prophet. They said: "Testify [Jesus], that we are Muslims"' (5:111). Sura Five provides several views of Jesus that are in contrast to the Gospels and will be discussed later.

Abraham, the first Hanif

Abraham, his son Ishmael, Jacob and his children, the twelve tribes, the prophets Moses and Jonah, even the pharaoh, Solomon the wise, the Twelve Apostles of Jesus, as well as the different sects and parties, are described in the Qur'an as Muslims. It is incumbent on all to join with Muhammad and all Muslims and to repeat the frequent appeal given in the Qur'an: "Say: we believe in God" (2:136).

Muhammad instructs his followers to avoid divisions like the children of Israel, to unite their tribes, to believe in God and to die in Islam, wherein there is unity, reconciliation and peace. The Qur'an warns, "Believers! If you listen to a faction within the People of the Book, they would render you apostates" (3:100). According to this verse, along with others, anyone who believes in God and in his books and does not try to make any difference between his prophets will be a true Muslim (3:84).

Muslims before Islam

"When it is recited to them, they say: We believe therein, for it is the truth from our Lord: Indeed we have been Muslims from before this" (28:53).

"He is who has named you Muslims, both before and in this (Qur'an)" (22:78).

"Knowledge was bestowed on us in advance of this, and we have submitted to God (in Islam)" (27:42).

"Who is better in speech than one who calls to God, works righteousness, and says: I am of those who bow in Islam" (41:33).

The good and true Muslim is one who believes in one God, respects the teachings of the Torah, the Gospel and the Qur'an. In addition to this belief one must believe in the message of all former prophets without making any distinctions between them. Muslims, according to the Qur'an, are those who bring unity and are not of those who divide into factions. They are those who accept the whole Book. Muslims are also those who look for peace and concord between sects without siding with one of them.

The word 'Islam' and its cognates are repeated seventy-one times in the Qur'an. It never describes a religion that is independent of the other revealed books. The former Islam identifies these four characteristics which are shared with the Islam that came with Muhammad's revelations. They both (1) do not differ between apostles and former prophets; (2) do emphasize the Unity of God while denying that God has partners; (3) seek unification for all sects and partisans within the Children of Israel and the People of the Book; and (4) make no distinctions between teachings from the Qur'an, the Gospel, and the Torah.

Muhammad makes every effort to trace Islam back to Abraham by linking it to his Muslim faith based upon his Hanifiyyah knowledge. When he establishes this linkage, he promotes Islam as the religion antecedent both to Judaism and Christianity. The Qur'an's teachings remind its readers of the Pentateuch and the Gospel. The Qur'an then acts to spur the Arabs to overcome the ideological conflicts prevailing at that time between the Jewish and Christian sects.

The Arab tribes, polytheists to a degree but claiming monotheism, were divided by these religious conflicts. In order to alleviate this situation, Muhammad tries to connect with a religion which already existed before any emergence of religious violence in Mecca. The links of Islam to Abraham is through the Hanif school set out by Waraqa. "Abraham was neither Jew nor Christian, he was a Hanif Muslim" (3:67).

Before any serious religious war or lesser conflict, Muhammad sees that the mission of Islam is to return to the basic creed of Abraham. This creed is the belief in one God and the recognition of absolute monotheism. Islam is exclusively based on this creed since the only sin recognized in Islam is the negation of this creed. Any other dereliction is forgivable. "God will not forgive the crime of idolatry but he will forgive all other sins" (4:48,116). The Qur'an repeats again and again: "There is no divinity than God;" "There is no other God than He;" "There is no God than the unique God;" "You would never have an other God" (3:18; 2:163; 5:116).

Muhammad Restrains Christian Dissensions

Muhammad, in his attempt to restrain possible dissension among Nazarenes and other Christians regarding Jesus Christ, moves toward the pure monotheism of Abraham. He rejects the divine Sonship of Christ and the redemptive meaning of Jesus' death, his crucifixion and his resurrection. Muhammad prefers removing any obstacle standing in the way of the absolute monotheism recognized by both the People of the Book, confessions and sects. The main objective is to suppress Arab dissension and possible conflicts with those who have a different view of monotheism regarding Jesus Christ.

The Prophet Muhammad himself puts his mission squarely on the line to support both the prior Islam and its new revelation. He declares that he belongs to that prior Islam, establishing its teachings and guiding its followers. Is it a divine command or an instruction given by Waraqa directly to him? Here is his partial answer: "I am commanded to be of those who are Muslims" (27:91). "I have been commanded to bow (in Islam) to the Lord of the Worlds" (40:66).

There are further claims placed upon Muhammad. Is it God, or is it the priest Waraqa who asks him to be the leader of Meccan Muslims, their Imam prayer leader. He will become much like a lord who would be responsible as the civil commander and protector. He will act as their primate. "I am commanded to be the first among Muslims" (39:12; 6:14). "This am I commanded and I am the first of those who bow to his will" (6:163).

This primacy is not strictly a temporal authority despite its statutory and hierarchical character, but rather it points to another world influence and responsibility. In fact, the Qur'an itself excludes openly such temporal primacy. It recognizes and confirms the existence of Islam prior to Muhammad and the Islam of all the prophets before that of the Arabs.

What then is the nature of this Islam which was prior to the Arab Islam? Islam is not different from a form of Nosrania, the Ebionite Christian sect that was in Mecca. Arab Islam is a reflection of the earlier seventh century Arab monotheism. A follower of Islam believes in its Haniffiya roots by honoring previous Scriptures. The previous Scriptures call upon the current recipients of the new revelation to observe all the former precepts.

Chapter VII

Hanif and Nosrania in Early Islam

The prior existence of Arab Islam is testified by Muhammad's attachment to Abraham's religion, called al-Hanafiyyah. The word Hanif (pl. Hunafa') is repeated in twelve Qur'anic verses. Some of them are Meccan and others are from the revelations that came when Muhammad was in Medina, 622 to 632 AD.[1] The message of the Hanafiyyah calls for a strict monotheism while denouncing polytheism and idolatry. The same word is sometimes used as an attribute of the immutable religion of the straight path.

The True Religion

The following descriptions are a summary of the faith and practices of the Hanifiyyah that Waraqa inherits from his ancestors and passes along to his protégé Muhammad.

Al-Hanif is a description of Abraham, his religion and his followers who never made other creatures as partners with God and who do not know disputations or schisms. They practiced "the standard religion" (98:5) or "the true religion" meaning they believed in one God.

Al-Hanif is the quality of that one who forsakes polytheism and idolatry, keeps distance with quarrels emerging inside a religion or a creed, avoids infamy and idolatry and abstains from any fallacy and calumny (22:30,31).

Al-Hanif is that one who worships God by negating all other gods, practices his prayers and pays al-zakat (98:5), submits himself to God, gives alms (4:125), and believes in God alone without association of other divinities (30:30,31). Al-Hanif is that one who is faithful. He is "from God's nature which is given to human beings" (30:30). It is a simple, unchanging faith. Abraham, as a "friend of God" (Exodus 33:11) is a model of obedience and submission (4:125).

The Hanafite religion is not an independent one during Muhammad's life but existed in pre-Qur'anic time, as did Christianity, Judaism, Mazdeanism and Sabeanism. Yet the expression al-Hanif (the pious) is the quality of a religion or the attribute of Abraham's faith in one God. Grammatically, it is used in all verses as an attribute and not as substantive.

The Hanif Faith of Abraham

Al-Hunafa' are those who follow Abraham's creed (22:31). God "has guided him on the straight path" (98:5). Al-Hanafiyyah is an attribute of Abraham's religion, as well as of that of Muhammad. "It is the cult of your father Abraham, it is he who named you Muslims, both before the Qur'an and in the Qur'an" (22:77,78). Abraham was the first of the Hunafa'. Muhammad is the first Muslim. And Abraham was like Muhammad, "a pious Muslim" (a Hanif)(3:67).

Alongside the Qur'an's mentioning of the al-Hanafiyyah, there are other reports that cover the Hunafa' groups that are listed in several Compilers' documents.[2] These records, considered together, recognize the Hunafa' as an Arab non-idolatrous religious body that predated Islam. They condemned all potential heresies at a time when there were widespread disputes about the nature of Abraham's attack on idols. The Compilers of the various Sirahs underline Muhammad's adherence to al-Hanafiyyah which they consider tolerant in contrast to the Jews "who twist their tongues and slander the faith (4:46)." According to the following hadith, Muhammad said, "I have announced a tolerant and easy religion."[3] "The religion which is most pleasing to God is that which is pious and tolerant."[4] "I did not announce either Judaism - nor Nosrania, but the pious and tolerant religion."[5]

We note here the adding of the word "Nosrania" in the last hadith which does not exist in previous sayings. It is very likely to have been added later because Muslims always considered tolerance as one of the most important qualities of the various Nazarene faiths. The words in this hadith fit a later time of the Islamic conquests, when Muslims begin to assume hostile and aggressive attitudes against all Christians including their early ally, the Nosrania. If the Hanafite religion is considered tolerant, as was the Nosrania, that would mean Muhammad considered both as one and the same tolerant religion.

Other characteristics of Hanifiyyah are mentioned in the life stories of Muhammad. Males should be circumcised and ready to go on pilgrimage.[6] A believer assumes the creed of Abraham and follows him.[7] A Hanif believer gives up idols and washes himself of sins.[8] He abstains from eating pagan meat and from drinking alcohol.[9] In this context al-Tabari reports, "The people of Modar who went on pilgrimage to al-Ka'ba at the time of Jahiliyyah were called 'Hunafa'."[10] Unity of Hanifiyyah and Nosrania is also a part of the Compiler records and repeated in legends about some Hunafa' and Nazarene priests and monks.

Waraqa Ibn Nawfal joins two other priests, Ibn Saida and 'Uthman al-Huwayrith, as part of a Hanafiyyah group. They have been identified as being Arabs converted to Nosrania and Hunafa'. In another hadith, Muhammad is speaking of the priest Ibn Sa'idah as a "man from 'Ayad. He became a Hanif in the Jahiliyyah era."[11] In Muruj al-Zahab (The Golden Meads), al-Mass'ud reports, "Hanzalah b. Safwan, Khalid b. Sinan al-Absi, Ri'ab al-Shafi, al-Qiss Ibn Sa'idah, Umayyah b. Abi al-Salt al-Thaqafi, al-Qiss Waraqa b. Nawfal, 'Addass al-Qubayss, Sarma abi Uns al-Ansari, Abi 'Amir al-Oussi, Abdallah b. Jahsh and al-Qiss Buhayrah... were all Hunafa' (pious) as they were Nosrania."[12]

The word Hanafiyyah was a favorable attribute applied both to Arab Nosrania and to the One-God followers prior to Islam. Abraham was a "Muslim Hanif" (4:125). "He is who the Lord led in the straight path and became Hanif" (6:161). "Whoever prays and is charitable is Hanif" (98:5). The significant thing here is that a Hanif may be both a Nosrania and a Muslim. Subsequently, Nosrania, Hanafiyyah and Islam are three names that merged within a short time after the death of Muhammad.

In referring to the Qur'an, biographies and Compilers' documents we find Muhammad's attitudes regarding the People of the Book. These Jews, Christians and local Nosrania all belong to this category. Now let us take a close examination of the Qur'anic sayings concerning each of these bodies on how they responded to Muhammad's new revelations. There were those who rejected it as a divine announcement and there were those who accepted it. Indeed, four groups are a concern of the Qur'an: Jews, Christians, Nosrania and the Hanifa', the "pious" among preIslamic Arabs. Identification of each of their creeds and their attitudes toward the new revelation of Islam will provide a glimpse of what Muhammad announced as the "constant religion."

Three of these are mentioned below with Islam added to compare with the other monotheistic faiths.

The Jews

There are those among the Jews who honor what has been revealed to their fathers, yet do not believe in anything else. Muhammad invites them to believe in what has been revealed to him, but they firmly decline his appeal. "When it is said to them: Believe in what God has sent down, they say: 'We believe in what was sent down to us.' And they reject all besides" (2:91).

"When it is said to them, 'Follow the law God has sent you,' they say, 'We follow the traditions of our fathers'" (2:170); "When it is said to them: 'Come to what God has revealed to his apostle,' they say, 'Sufficient for us are the ways we found our fathers following'" (5:104). "When it is said to them: 'Follow what God has sent down', they say: 'Nay, we shall follow the ways we found our fathers following'" (31:21).

Muhammad assails the unbelievers who reject his message as "the evil of humanity" (*Sharr al-bariyyah*) (98:6). The children of Israel are warned not to be "the first who decline his appeal" (2:41). "They are fond of listening to falsehood" (5:42). "The Jews are those who displace words from their correct places" (4:46). The Qur'an blames them because they were unsatisfied with what was revealed to them. "Is it not enough for them that we sent down to you the book which is rehearsed to them?" (29:51) which they ignore even when it is in their hands! "We have revealed to you a book in which is a message for you: Will you not then understand?" (21:10).

He openly accuses them of unbelief (*kufr*). "They are those who, among the People of the Book, are leading in unbelief" (2:121) and "they do not believe in miracles" (59:2). They enjoy betraying the people. "Some party among the People of the Book will bring you back to unbelief" (2:109). "Some party of the People of the Book would like to corrupt you" (3:69). "They clothe truth with falsehood" (3:71). "They obstruct those who believe from the path of God" (3:99). The Qur'an reproaches the Jews for their non-acceptance of the entirety of the books from the Pentateuch and the Gospel. "Have you not turned your vision to those who were given a portion of the book, they traffic in error" (4:44). "Have you not seen those who have been given a portion of the Book of God to settle their disputes, but a party of them turn back and decline (the arbitration)" (3:23).

However, the direct contact between Muhammad and Jews did not take place until 622 AD in the city of Medina. Their presence, as well as their influence, in Mecca was insignificant. In Meccan verses, we do not find, as in the Medinan verses, the same attitude against Jews. Meccan verses do not report anything about them. Even their name is not mentioned in the earlier chapters of the Qur'an. Muhammad has no reason to consider them in Mecca as enemies, as was the case in Medina. In the latter city, the hostilities that arose between Muhammad and Jews were sharp and often treacherous.

Biographical, historical, geographic and commentary documents, as well as the collection of hadiths, abound on this topic. They extend all efforts to contrive tales about conflicts between Arabs and Jews reminding all of the numerous enmities that existed between the Jews and the Muslims. They relate to details of several events. Like the exergue on coins, the hatred between Arabs and Jews is stamped widely throughout this Arabic region. Even pagan priests, Nosrania priests and some Arab south-soothsayers remind Muhammad of the Jewish hostility against him and his mission. All these facts were a part of conditions prevailing particularly in Medina but not in Mecca. It is necessary to mention this fact, for it allows a better understanding of the Qur'an's own story about the prophet's mission to his Arab brethren.

Christians

Muhammad did not effectively know the Christians. He ever ignored the existence of their official books and the nature of their faith. Most Christians at the time of the Qur'an's first appearances believed in the Gospel with four versions, in Christ's divinity and his divine filiation. The orthodox nature of Christ was agreed at the council of Nicaea (325 AD) but there existed widespread opposition to various creeds and to the attempts to set up a Constantine type church state. Because of the divisions, the Church of the East, as well as the Latin Roman Catholic church in the West, were divided in groups and parties. Arabs were in contact with some of these groups, like Jacobites, Nestorians and Melkites. However, all these groups recognized Christ's divinity, his crucifixion, as well as the mysteries of Resurrection and Redemption.

Muhammad reproaches the Christians for excessive attitudes issuing from their creeds about Jesus Christ and Trinity. The non-Trinitarian sects like the Nosrania in Mecca opposed these Trinitarian Christians. The Qur'an's People of the Book could have been a mixture of sectarian Jews and Nosrania Christians but more likely they were Christians from South and North Arabia. These Trinitarian Christians stood in opposition to the Jews who did not recognize Christ's prophetic ministry. The Qur'an's later chapters consider them, "the extremists in religion" and give them the following advice: "O People of the Book! Commit no excesses in your religion, nor say of God ought but the truth" (4:171).

"The Messiah, Jesus son of Mary, is the Apostle of God and his Word which he bestowed on Mary and a spirit proceeding from God. So believe in God and his apostles. Say not, 'Trinity.' Desist. It will be better for you: for God is one God. For exalted is He above having a son. To him belong all things in the heavens and on earth. The Messiah does not disdain to serve and worship God..." (4:171, 172). The warnings are specifically addressed to Christians apart from the local Nosrania sect. "O People of the Book! Do not exceed in your religion the bounds trespassing beyond the truth" (5:77).

However, the Qur'an does not indulge in wasting advice when it pours forth condemnations:

"They do blaspheme who say: God is the Messiah, the son of Mary. But the Messiah said: O children of Israel! Worship God, my Lord and your Lord. Whoever joins other gods to God, God will forbid him the paradise, and the fire will be his abode... They do blaspheme who say: God is one of three in a Trinity. There is no god except one God. The Messiah, son of Mary, is no more than an Apostle. Many were apostles that passed away before him. His mother was a woman of truth. They had both to eat daily food" (5:73-75).

Those Christians Muhammad met during the last years of his life were part of a delegation from the South Arabian city of Najran. They came to discern what was going on in Medina with Muhammad at the head of the Muslims. He grants them peace while they are holding their discussions. On that occasion, however, he seizes an opportunity for conducting a debate with them about Jesus' divinity and his sonship.   Three Suras recall the conversations with these Trinitarian Arab delegates: (3:33-64; 4:170-176; 5:75-80,112-122). In Sura 9, one finds the same attitude toward Christians, relating again the formal hostility against them in what was the last chapter in the Qur'an.

Nosrania

Nosrania believers are different than the Jews and Christians. They do not reject Jesus' prophecy as do the Jews and they do not believe in his divine nature, as do the Najran Christians. They occupy, according to the Qur'an, an intermediary position (2:143), and a blessed place (5:66). They claim to observe all the book (3:199), including the Pentateuch and the Gospel. They believe both in Moses and in Jesus Christ. They are a group of the People of the Book who uphold in what is revealed (3:72) and "rehearse the signs of God" (3:183). They ardently worship the one God. "Among the People of the Book there are certainly those who believe in God and in the book sent to you, if entrusted with a hoard of gold, will readily pay it back" (3:75).

Nosrania, People of Knowledge

"Those who are firmly grounded in knowledge say: We believe in the Book, the whole of it is from our Lord" (3:7). "Those endued with knowledge" (3:18). "Those who were given knowledge beforehand (the Qur'an), when it is recited to them, fall down on their faces" (17:107). "Those who have received knowledge know that the Qur'an is a truth given by the Lord, so that they believe" (22:54). "Those to whom knowledge has come see that the revelation sent down to you from your Lord is the Truth" (34:6).

The Nosrania sectarians possess "evident signs who received knowledge" (29:49). "They exult in such knowledge as they have" (40:83). "The Lord will raise up those of you who (the Arabs) believe and who have been granted mystic knowledge" (58:11).

Muhammad asks those with the special knowledge of the book to witness to the veracity of his mission and his book. They are, with God and angels, witnesses of monotheism. They accept the order and the sign of Creation (3:190). Nosrania believers witness to the

Qur'an, because the content of this book is corresponding with that of their own book. "A witness from among the children of Israel testifies to its (the Qur'an) similarity and they believe" (46:9).

Muhammad is satisfied with their compliance. "Say, 'Enough for a witness between you and me is God, and such as have knowledge of the book'" (13:43). When he faces doubts of what he has received, he questions them to confirm his message. "If you are in doubt as to what we have revealed unto you, then ask those who have been reading the book from before you" (10:94). Even when Muhammad's fellows doubt his mission, he orders them, "Ask the men of Scriptures, if you do not realize it" (16:43). When he finds difficulty to express his argument, he himself seeks arbitration: "Let the People of the Book judge by what God has revealed therein" (5:47).

Muslims

Muhammad's mission consists in unifying Nosrania divisions. So he commands them, "Be steadfast in religion and make no divisions therein" (42:13). "Hold fast, all together, by the rope which God stretches out for you, and be not divided among yourselves" (3:103).

He is haunted by the idea that he could be responsible for their conflicts. "Truly I feared that you should say: you have caused a division among the Children of Israel" (20:94). God informs him, "As far as those who divide their religion and break up into sects, you have no part in them" (6:159). Muhammad replies to God's appeal. "We make no difference between one and another among them, and to God bow we our will (in Islam). If anyone desires a religion other than Islam, it will never be accepted of him" (3:85). He repeats later, "We make no distinction between one and another of his apostles" (2:285).

Muhammad describes his followers, "They are those who believe in God and in his apostles and do not make distinctions among them" (4:152). He advises them, "Be not among those who join gods to God, those who split up their religion and became sects" (30:30,31). "Be not like those who after receiving clear signs, are divided among themselves and fall into disputations" (3:105).

The Nosrania and Muslims became unified by the name, by the book and the faith, so that they became "a unique nation" (23:52). Their name becomes "Muslims" now expanded to mean those who unify and do not divide. Their book is the Qur'an, their faith is Islam i.e., the religion that unifies all sects under one immutable doctrine and their creed says: "There is no other divinity than Allah (God)" (3:18). In this regard the disciples of Jesus, the apostles, seek the testimony of Jesus confirming that they are truly Muslims. "The disciples said, 'We are God's helpers. We believe in God and do you [Jesus] bear witness that we are Muslims?'" (3:52)

It is evident that the Muslims, once the Nosrania community, united in one group now anticipate the disappearance of all sects and parties. The faithful remnants that believe in the message of the Prophet Muhammad join the Muslims to be absorbed into Islam. This is due to the fact that Muhammad first supports the Nosrania when others turned against them (61:14). They become the standard for the Arabic religion even while "most among mankind do not understand" (30:30).

Those who most fiercely resist this new religion are first the Jews who mix truth with falsehood and conceal it. "O People of the Book! Why do you clothe the Truth with falsehood?" (3:71). Later when Christians resist, they, too, are considered as being outside the true religion because the Christians exaggerated in their creeds about the truth (4:71). The "hypocrite" Arabs are excluded from this new religion, because they keep aloof from the Messenger and are dealing too much with their wealth and physical heritage. They are "the worst in unbelief and hypocrisy" (9:97).

Only one group prevails among the People of the Book and the children of Israel. They believe in God and in all his Books. They are faithful to the straight path of the standard and true religion. "They worship God, offering him sincere devotions, being true, establishing regular prayers and practicing regular charity" (98:5). "This is the true religion" (9:33). "God commands you not to worship another god than God. This is the straight path" (12:40). He who does not obey will be considered among the losers. "Set your face to the straight religion before God comes on the day when there is no chance for averting" (30:43).

Chapter VIII

Birth Narratives of Jesus and His Mother

The case has been made for many similarities between the Qur'an and previous scriptures such as the Pentateuch and the Gospels. These Qur'anic similarities have their counterparts in either the canonical, or biblical or apocryphal versions. It is possible to trace some oral traditions and popular legends that have grown out of the Hebraic-Christian heritage and found their way into popular Muslim traditions.[1]

The Qur'an evokes a certain vision of God and his attributes that stems directly from the older holy books and is filled with events and characters that can only be understood with knowledge of the Bible. This list of common subject matter is long and begins with the creation's story (Genesis 1 and 2) and Adam and Eve. Other Old Testament personages become prophets in the Qur'an. They include Noah and the deluge; Abraham and his two sons, Isaac and Ishmael; Joseph and his sojourn in Egypt; Moses, as God's interlocutor and the Pentateuch's father; King David and the psalms; Solomon the wise; the patient Job. Among some non-biblical legends are tales of 'Aad, Thamud and the land of Sheba that relate to specific Arab topics.

The New Testament is represented with an expanded view of John, son of Zechariah, and his birth; the birth of Mary, mother of Jesus, and the Qur'anic interpretations of her uniqueness. These subjects find their sources in Jewish and Christian books that were available to the Meccan Nosrania church.

Jesus Christ

Jesus and Mary, his mother, represent the widest divergence between Islam and Judaism as the Jews reject Jesus' prophetic ministry including his supernatural birth. The majority of the Christians of the seventh century accepted Jesus' divine nature while a few isolated groups like the Meccan Nosrania resisted the biblical and creedal statements of Jesus' divine sonship. Islam came to agree with this sectarian view that was part of Waraqa's teaching in Mecca.

The Messiah in the Qur'an is "Jesus ('Isa) son of Mary (Miryam), an ordinary human being" (4:171). God creates him, like Adam, "from dust" (3:59), but in a miraculous manner (3:45; 19:34,35). This conception is identical with that of Ebionists who believe that the Messiah is "Jesus, son of Mary" (19:16-22).

Although the Messiah is a human being, he is also an apostle. "Other apostles preceded him" (5:75). But he is superior to all prophets, because he is "strengthened by the Holy Spirit" (2:87). John 1:1 proclaims him to be "the Word of God" while the Qur'an identifies Jesus as "a spirit from Him" (4:171). God grants him obvious signs and the power to do miracles. Jesus starts speaking when he is still in infancy (19:29). "He created from mud a bird's face" and he healed "a man born blind and a leper, and called out the dead from their tombs" (5:110).

Justin Martyr, the second century Christian apologist, records that the Ebionist view of the Messiah "is the most memorable among all prophets and embodied an evangelical spirit."[2] Later Origen says that the Ebionite conception of Jesus was initially not a Messiah but "he became by choice," earning the Messiahship by his completing the law.[3] Another Christian Father, Irenaeus, states the Ebionite position: "No other person than Jesus has completed the law. If another did what is written in the law, he should become the Messiah."[4] For this reason, the Ebionists do not recognize the Messiah's divinity, because he is not born from God according to Origen.[5] However, the largely Jewish-Christian Ebionists attribute to Jesus the power for making miracles. Some recall episodes from the official Gospels like the healing of a leper, a blind man, and the resurrection of a dead person. But other events like creating a bird from mud are only mentioned in their own books.

In the Qur'an, any divine role for Jesus, the Messiah, is absolutely condemned because "God never fathered and has never been fathered" (112:3). The Qur'an adds, "The Messiah does not disdain to serve and worship God, nor do the angels, those nearest to God"

(4:172). Although Jesus may be one who "is among those nearest to God" (3:45) yet "God may destroy him" (5:17).

This attitude is similar to that of the heterodoxy of the Ebionists as described by Epiphanius who writes: "The Messiah is not born from God, the father, he is created. He reigns over angels and over all works of the Almighty." Epiphanius continues, "In their point of view, the Messiah is nothing other than an angel" or "the first among their heads."[6] A cryptic description provided by one of the earliest Christian authors, the Shepherd of Hermas, recalls the creation of angels. "When God liked to create the angels near fire on number 7, he decided that one of them should be his son."[7]

Ebionists believe that "the Messiah came down on Jesus the day of his baptism in Jordan, and left him before his martyrdom."[8] One of the apocryphal writers maintains, "When Jesus has been crucified, the Messiah left Jesus, son of Mary, just before his death on the cross."[9]

Both Saints, Irenaeus and Epiphanius, assert what the Ebionites believe. "The Messiah transforms himself voluntarily in different forms. By his crucifixion, he transformed himself into Simeon who is crucified in his place, whereas he has been raised alive to the one who sent him down. Then Jesus makes sport of those who betrayed him in order to be arrested, because he was invisible for all."[10] Irenaeus reasons that if they consider Christ's "death as mysterious, and his resurrection as elevation to heaven, he could not have the quality of a Redeemer nor of a Savior."[11]

The Qur'an indicates that Jesus was saved from the crucifixion and taken directly to be with God (3:55). The Messiah has been neither killed nor crucified, but he looked so for people who have claimed that they killed Jesus. "We (the Jews boast) killed Christ Jesus, the son of Mary. No, they did not kill him, nor crucified him, but so it was made to appear to them" (4:157). Here the Suras show that God has in turn made sport of them because he is the "best of all those who plot (*al-makireen*)" (3:54; 13:42).

The Qur'an does not say that Jesus Christ has been resuscitated from death by his own power, as the Christians of Antioch and Rome believe in this post Nicene era. "Such was Jesus, the son of Mary, it is a statement of truth about which they vainly dispute" (19:34).

Mary, mother of Jesus

Qur'anic and Nosrania accounts of Mary, mother of Jesus, often coincide. They do not agree with Jews who are accused of false witness against Mary (4:156).

However, Mary takes a privileged place in the Qur'an. Her name is the only female who is mentioned in this book. The appellation, "Jesus son of Mary ('Isa Ibn Miryam)," is used in the Qur'an, contrary to typical Semitic names that attribute the son to his father never to a mother. This exception in the Qur'an is deliberate. It aims at highlighting the miraculous birth of Jesus.   The name of Mary is repeated thirty-four times in the Qur'an where she and her son are designated "signs of God" (23:50).

The Qur'an and the Nosrania documents recognize the esteem which God held for Mary's fathers and their heritage. She provides respectful proofs like her virginity that honor her heritage.   This includes her belonging to the prophets' dynasty, from Adam and Noah to Abraham's family until 'Imran, (the family of Mary). "God has chosen Adam and Noah, the family of Abraham and that of 'Imran above all people, offspring one of the other... The woman of 'Imran said to the Lord: I dedicate unto you what is in my womb" (3:33,34).

The Birth of Mary Qur'anic Account

"A woman of 'Imran said: 'O my Lord! I do dedicate unto you what is in my womb for the special service" (3:35). "When she was delivered, she said: 'O my Lord! Behold! I am delivered of a female child!' - And God knew best what she brought forth - 'and nowise is the male like the female. I have named her Mary, and I commend her and her offspring to your protection from the evil one, the rejected.' Right graciously did her Lord accept her. He made her grow in purity and beauty" (3:36,37).

As far as the miraculous birth of Mary is concerned, the Qur'an and Nazarene sources provide some details that are not found in the canonical scriptures. The apocryphal Gospel of James sheds some light on the Qur'an versions of Mary's birth. "We read in the history of the twelve dynasties of Israel... so that the honor of the belonging of the Messiah and his mother Mary to Jacob's dynasty is revealed to us..."[12]

Mary's mother, Joanna, is introduced in the Gospel of James: "The Lord's angel said: 'Joanna, Joanna! God has heard your prayer. You will conceive and give birth. It will be spoken about your posterity around the world.' Joanna replied, 'The Lord is alive. If I have a boy or a daughter, I will present him or her to God, the Lord. He or she will be at the Lord's service all of his or her life.' After Mary's birth, Joanna asked the midwife, 'To what did I give birth?' The midwife answered, 'a girl.' Joanna gave to her daughter the name of Miryam (Mary).' Her father, Joachim, offered a prayer: 'Lord! Look to your daughter! Receive and bless her.' The girl grew day after day."[13]

The Qur'an follows Mary to the Jerusalem temple's entrance where she meets with the leaders far from the curious. Zechariah as the head of priests receives her and takes care of her. The Lord provides her with food. She remains in a seclusion and prayer until her wedding day.

The Qur'anic records continue, "Relate in the book the story of Mary, when she withdrew from her family to a place in the temple. She placed a screen (to shelter herself) from them" (19:17). Zechariah took care of the infant. Every time he entered her chamber to see her, he found her supplied with sustenance. He said: 'From where comes this to you?' She said: 'From God: for God provides sustenance to whom he pleases without measure'" (3:37). The word to Zechariah includes the news about the coming prophet, John the Baptist, (3:39) but Muhammad is included only by revelation from an event that does not appear elsewhere in the birth narratives. "You (Muhammad) were not with them when they cast lots with arrows as to which of them should be charged with the care of Mary" (3:44).

From the James Gospel, "Joachim conducts his daughter, Mary, to the Temple. She remains there for three years. An angel entrusts Zechariah, head of priests, to find a husband for her. So the wise people among Israel's children have been consulted... She obtains her food from the hand of Lord's angel."[14]

When Mary is in the Temple, the angel came and announced to her that she will give birth. The third Sura, titled "The Family of 'Imran," and the nineteenth Sura, called "Miryam," together cover the details of the announcements to Mary about the coming birth of a son.

"We sent to her our angel, and he appeared before her as a man in all respects" (19:17).

"The angels said to Mary: 'God has chosen you and purified you among the women of all nations'" (3:42).

"The angels said to Mary: 'God gives you glad tidings of a Word from Him: his name will be Messiah Jesus, the son of Mary, held in honor in this world and the hereafter, and one of the nearest confidants to God. He shall speak to the people in childhood and in maturity. He shall be of the company of the righteous'" (3:45,46).

Mary's responses according to the Qur'an reflect some of the Gospel's records. "Mary said: 'I seek refuge from you to God most gracious: come not near if you fear God'" (19:18).

Gabriel answers Mary's fears, " Nay, I am only a messenger from your Lord, to announce to you the gift of a holy son" (19:19).

"O my Lord!" replies Mary, "How shall I have a son when no man has touched me?" (3:47).

This is added from Sura 19, "... and I am not unchaste?'" (19:20).

"The angel said: 'God creates what he will. He said: 'Be,' and it is'" (3:47).

Gabriel reassures Mary, "So it will be. Your Lord said: 'That is easy for me. He will be a Sign unto men and a mercy from us. It is a matter so decreed'" (19:21).

Previous to these Qur'anic announcements to Mary with her responses, we have the Gospel of Luke's account and more from the apocryphal Gospel of James. From the latter, "God sent angel Gabriel to the Virgin. He tells her: 'Be blessed! You find a grace by God. You will conceive his Word. He will be the Son of the Highest. You will name him: Jesus.'"[15] The Lukan message also identifies Gabriel as the messenger who met Mary to announce that she would be the mother of a blessed son.

"Gabriel appeared to her and said: Congratulations favored lady! The Lord is with you!" (Luke 1:28). Confused and disturbed, Mary tried to think what the angel could mean (Luke 1:28).

Then the angel tells her: "Do not be frightened, for God has decided to wonderfully bless you" (Luke 1:30). Mary asks the angel, "But how can I have a baby? I am a virgin, no man has touched me" (Luke 1:34). The angel replies, "the Holy Spirit shall come upon you, and the power of God shall overshadow you; so the baby born to you will be utterly holy and called the son of God" (Luke 1:35). Mary's humble answer to all of this, "I am the Lord's servant, and I am willing to do whatever He wants" (Luke 1:38).

When the birth pains come, the Qur'an continues, "she withdrew to a far place" (19:22) in a grassy area where she found a palm tree under which she waited for her baby. Immediately after, "someone cried from above: 'Do not sorrow! Your Lord turned a stream on your feet'" (19:24). Commentaries do not agree about the person who called out to Mary. Is the voice from her baby or an angel? The Qur'anic text is not clear, but this story and that of Hagar and her son, Ishmael, allows a comparison with this text and the one in Genesis 15. Mary is informed through an angel, much as an angel has informed Hagar centuries earlier.

The Genesis Account of Hagar's Rescue

"When the water was gone she [Hagar] left her son in the shade of a bush and went off and sat down a hundred yards or so away. 'I don't want to watch him die,' she said, and burst into tears, sobbing wildly. Then God heard the boy crying, and the angel of God called Hagar from heaven:

'Hagar, what is the matter? Don't be afraid! For God has heard the lad's cries as he is lying there. Go and get him and comfort him...' Then God opened her eyes and she saw a well; so she refilled the skin and gave the lad a drink. And God blessed the boy" (Genesis 21:14-20).

Jesus' birthplace in the Qur'an has a good likeness to the birth of Ishmael. It is neither a "cradle" (Luke 2:7), nor "in a cave" but in a meadow. That is much like Ishmael's birth near where the angel of the Lord found a well to drink water (Genesis 16:7). The Qur'anic outdoor images of the birth of Jesus include a stream and a palm tree (19:24,25). An angel directs Mary to shake the palm to make the dates accessible.

"And the pains of childbirth drove her to the trunk of a palm-tree. She cried: 'Ah! Would that I had died before this! Would that I have been a thing forgotten and out of sight!' (19:23). But a voice cried to her from beneath the palm-tree: 'Grieve not! For your Lord has provided a rivulet beneath you. Shake toward yourself the trunk of the palm-tree: it will let fall fresh ripe dates upon you'" (19:24,25). A similar story from non-biblical James Gospel that was available to Waraqa which states, "The palm-tree bent in front of Mary and presented to her delicious fruits to feed her lad during her trip to Egypt."[16]

The Qur'anic version of Mary provides the impression that Mary's chastity is well known. Zechariah directs his words to Mary, "O sister of Aaron! Your father was not a man of evil, nor your mother a woman unchaste" (19:28). Mary is obliged to ask her son to lighten the weight of people's accusations. Zechariah speaks again, "I am indeed the servant of God: he has given me revelation and made me a prophet. He has made me blessed wherever I be ... Peace is on me the day I was born..." (19:30,33).

The Holy Spirit

In Hebrew Scriptures revelation has been attributed at times to God and other times to angels. The Pentateuch's texts use both sources. In Genesis, Jacob speaks, "The angel of God told me in a dream: 'Jacob!' and I answered: 'Yes.' He said: 'Open your eyes and look. I am the God you met at Bethel...'" (Genesis 31:1-13). The book of Judges says, "The angel of God arrived... and announced: I brought you out of Egypt into the land which I promised to your ancestors. And I said that I would never break my covenant with you" (Judges 2:1-4). The book of Exodus reads, "Suddenly the angel of Jehovah appeared to him as a flame of fire in a bush... and God called out to him" (Exodus 3:2-4). The book of Acts of Apostles interchanges these two terms, "The angel of the Lord said to Philip... The Holy Spirit said to "Philip..." (Acts 8:26,29).

Who is the Lord's angel in all these scriptures? Is he an autonomous being independent of God or is he God himself?

This combination of a divine with a human messenger is also found in the Qur'an. But there the amalgam is the angel Gabriel and the Holy Ghost. "We gave Jesus the son of Mary clear signs (about his mission) and strengthened him with the Holy Spirit" (2:87), that means the spirit of God, as it is quoted in the Pentateuch. But in other verses, angel Gabriel is clearly identified. "Say, the Holy Spirit has brought the revelation from your Lord" (16:102). "The Spirit of Faith brought it from heaven" (26:193). Gabriel is definitely the angel associated with revelation. "Verily this is the word of a most honorable messenger (angel Gabriel), endued with power, with rank before the Lord of the

Throne, with authority there, and faithful to his trust" (81:19-21). "By God's will, Gabriel brings down the revelation to your heart" (2:97).

There is a curious blending of the Holy Spirit and Mary at the birth of Jesus in Nazarene and Nosrania documents. Origen quotes what is said about Jesus Christ in the Hebrew Gospel: "My mother, the Holy Spirit, brought me."[17] Jerome explains that by saying:, "That is a proof of their creed (that of Ebionists) that the Holy Spirit is the Christ's mother."[18]

There is a linguistic explanation that highlights the feminine nature of the Holy Spirit, which is attributed to the pen of al-Ya'qubi. "When Jesus has been baptized, the Holy Spirit came out on water." The verb "came out" is in the Arabic feminine case: *kharajat* as it is reported in Jerome's references to the Hebrew Gospel that Waraqa later translated into Arabic. "The Holy Spirit applies to Jesus at the time of his baptism. She says: 'Thou are my lovely son.'"[19] Aphrahate, one of the eminent scholars in the Aramaic Syriac Church, adds this, "The man loves God his father and the Holy Spirit his mother."[20]

A final note regarding Jesus and his relationship to God arises in the Qur'an when God actually reproaches Jesus. God inquires of Jesus, "Did you ever say to the people: 'Take, as gods, me and my mother rather than the one God?'" (5:116). This is the response to the beliefs of some Christians who venerated the Virgin Mary and glorified her name beyond what the Bible would warrant. In certain cases others presented offerings to her. But this minority did not include the Meccan Nosrania who did not promote any worship of Mary or her son, Jesus, the Messiah.

Chapter IX

Common Obligations and Rituals

The five Islamic pillars of religion--confession, daily prayers, alms, fasting and pilgrimage--may all be traced to the previous monotheistic faiths. Even the Gospels practiced these obligations and scores of others as prescribed by the teachings of the Pentateuch and the Talmud. Islam in general, and the Qur'an specifically, are depositories of religious duties as mediated through the Nosrania sect and the teaching of Waraqa. This chapter will highlight some of the pertinent items that are introduced in the earlier scriptures and incorporated into the Qur'an.

Circumcision

Circumcision is the sign testifying to God's alliance with human beings. It reminds a man of his organic membership with the covenant people of God. The ancient prophets considered it a basic part of divine law established in the Pentateuch (Exodus 12:44; Leviticus 12:3). Circumcision has been part of several cultures within and without the bounds of religious law. Several nations including the Assyrians, Egyptians and Arabs have interpreted this ritual as part of their social and religious cultures but records indicate that it was part of pagan services, as well.[1]

The Qur'an did not need to legislate circumcision as a religious practice. There are some hadiths in which Muhammad alludes to it: The Sahihs of al-Bukhari and Muslim are cited, "Circumcision is one of nature's qualities."[2] Another compiler says, "Circumcision is a law for men and a gratification for women."[3] Nazarenes and other Jewish Christians in all their diversities have observed this practice. For these Semites, circumcision was considered as basic to belief in the Messiah leading to salvation. In contrast to these believers, Christians from non-Jewish backgrounds under the teaching of the apostle Paul did not observe this rite as an entrance into faith in the Messiah (Acts of the Apostles 15:1-35; Galatians 2:11-21).

Al-Bukhari cites Heraclius, a famous astrologer who mentions a tradition of Muhammad in a response given to the astrologer's disciples: "One night by watching the stars I saw appearing 'the king of circumcision.'"[4] That was how Heraclius designated Muhammad at his birth and according to his vision Muhammad became "the king of circumcision." A similar designation is attached to Nazarene bishops when church historian, Eusebius, refers to them as "bishops of circumcision." He lists fifteen bishops with this title starting at the time of Christ until Trajan (d. 117). Eusebius notes, "These are the bishops of Jerusalem living between the Apostles' era and that already mentioned. All were circumcised."[5] The early Nazarene Church was called also "the Church of Circumcision."[6]

Ablutions and Purification

Ritual ablutions are part of the sacred obligations for Jews, Nazarenes and their co-religionists among the Nosrania and Muslims. Moses introduces this practice in the Pentateuch. The Jews wash themselves as part of worship ceremonies, namely before prayers, meals and religious ceremonies. Washing hands and feet is a duty for them "so that they do not die. It shall be a requirement forever to them, even to all generations" (Exodus 30:21). According to the Mosaic law found in Leviticus 14 and Numbers 19 the whole body should be washed under some prescribed circumstances. A man should wash himself in case of "flow from his body," or "if sperms drain from his body," or "if he has eaten a prey," or "if he has touched a bone or the body of a dead person or the tomb or the lepers." A woman is obliged to wash herself, "if blood runs from her body," or "if she is pregnant and is just giving birth ..." (Leviticus 15:3, 16, 33; Numbers 19:18; Matthew 8:4). These cases demand full body baths.

Ebionists and their offshoot Nosrania sectarians use the same practices. Epiphanius reports in this regard: "They practice daily entire ablutions for purification.... before meals and prayers and following any sexual intercourse."[7] Washing is a daily duty, but it also involves special cases such as after a snake's bite or when one is suffering from any sickness.[8]

Muslims must consider several conditions to cleanse themselves that involve either a major bath, which purifies the whole body, or a minor one, ablutions, to purify themselves. The Qur'an follows nearly identical procedures to those of Jews and Nazarenes before Islam. Believers are commanded, "Do not pray before doing your ablutions" (4:43). It specifies body parts that must be cleansed. "Believers! When you prepare for prayer, wash your faces, and your hands (and arms) to the elbows; rub your heads (with water) and wash your feet to the ankles. Clean yourselves after sexual intercourse" (5:6). Where there is no water, the Qur'an commends, "to clean the face and hands with earth" or "with pure and fine sand" (5:6) which Christians could use for baptism in the absence of water.

Prohibition on Alcohol

Alcohol is prohibited for Nazarene Ebionists but not for Jews and Christians. Ebionists forbade alcohol's uses even in their ceremonial offerings. According to Irenaeus, "Ebionists prohibit the mixture of heaven's wine with water. They use only water of this world."[9] In the Acts of Thomas, it says, "this offering is made with bread and water and without wine."[10] Clement of Alexandria comments, "Certain sects use in their offering bread and water instead of bread and wine, contrary to the Church's law."[11]

However, according to Origen, prohibited wine on earth will be legal in paradise.[12] Jesus says in Matthew's Gospel: "I tell you: I will never drink this wine until the day I drink it new with you in my Father's kingdom" (Matthew 26:29).

The alcoholic prohibition is mentioned in the Qur'an in which wine is considered "as an abomination created by Satan" (5:90) or as "the cause of a great sin" (2:219). Wine creates among the people "hate and enmity" (5:91). Conversely, all is legal in paradise where "run rivers of wine, a joy to those who drink" (47:15), where "people shall there exchange, one with another, a loving cup, free of frivolity, free of all taint of sin" (52:23). "Round about them will serve youth of perpetual freshness, with goblets, shining beakers, and cups filled out of clear-flowing wine which runs without interruption" (56:17,18). Certainly, "their thirst will be slaked with pure wine sealed" (83:25). Therefore prohibited alcohol on earth will be licit, welcomed in the Qur'anic paradise.

Prohibition of Pig Products

The pig is an unclean animal that Jews, the Nosrania and Muslims must avoid in all forms. The prohibition in the book of Moses forbids eating and touching swine. "You may not eat the pigs. You may not even touch the body of such animals, also they have cloven hooves" (Leviticus 11:7). Several Christian sects observed Moses' law at the beginning of the church in the Acts of the Apostles.[13] Jewish believers in the Messiah would continue to select foods based upon their previous faith. The Syriac Christians observed this prohibition of certain food. Aphrahate writes in this connection: "Because of your sins, God gave you animals destined to offerings and prohibited certain articles of food."[14]

Eventually, Christians abolished all food restrictions by accepting the words of Jesus when he said, "It is not what goes into the mouth that defiles a person but the things that come out defile him" (Mark 7:15).

As far as the Qur'an, it calls for the observance of Moses' law as well as much more of Jewish and Nazarene traditions. It prohibits some food and sanctifies some others that were once covered under the Mosaic laws. It repeats the prohibition on pork. "It is forbidden to you dead meat, and the flesh of swine, and that on which any other name has been invoked besides that of Allah" (2:173). The Qur'an emphasizes this prohibition several times (5:3; 6:145; 16:115).

Apostle Paul on Christian Liberty

"To this day, whenever Moses is read a veil lies over the minds of the Israelites; but when a man turns to the Lord the veil is removed. Now the Lord is the Spirit, and where the Spirit of the Lord is, there is liberty. We all, with unveiled face, beholding the glory of the Lord, are being changed into his likeness and from one degree of glory to another; for this comes from the Lord who is the Spirit" (II Corinthians 3:15-18).

Prohibition of Celibacy

The question of whether certain persons should abstain from marriage is already answered in Judaism and Nazarene communities. At the outset, it seems that the Ebionists observed celibacy. Epiphanius comments in this regard: "Nowadays they consider celibacy and marriage's abstention as illicit like similar sects. They prescribe marriage to people whereas they have respected formerly celibacy."[15]   In the words of another apocryphal writer, "He who abstains from getting married has to assume his own responsibility."[16]

The message of the Qur'an reveals no condemnation of celibacy as most would think. It does not proscribe, for example, monastic life absolutely. But it accuses monks "who did not follow monasticism as they should have done" (57:27). This Sura attacks those who do not behave in conformity with their vows. For this reason, the Qur'an at times praises the dedication of worthy monks who were "exempt from any conceit" (5:82). On other occasions, it brings charges against them who are bumptious and consume the people's goods. "They are indeed many among the priests and anchorites who in falsehood devour the substance of men and hinder them from the way of God" (9:34). Their bad behaviors motivate this accusation, for "they did not save at their disposal any of God's favors" (57:27).

Yet, the lingering attitude of the Qur'an toward monks and rabbis raised in the last, chronologically arranged, Sura is most damaging. The Christians "take their priests and their anchorites to be their lords in derogation of God. And they make Christ God" (9: 31). Once Muhammad's military conquests began there would no longer be any distinctions between Jews, Nazarenes and Christians.

Regarding marriage, it becomes almost compulsory in the Qur'an in comparison to other religious traditions. The Qur'an commends, "Marry women according to your pleasure, but if you fear that you shall not be able to deal justly with them, then marry one... Marry women of your choice, two, three or four." (4:3). "For fair in the eyes of men is the love of pleasures they covet, like women..." (3:14).

Fasting

Fasting is a common religious practice for all three monotheistic faiths. Qur'anic fasts are similar to those prevailing in Judaism and Nosrania sacred duties. The rabbinic Talmud gives the following details: "The outset of a fast day is the moment when man is able to distinguish the white thread from the blue one."[17] The Qur'an provides the same indicators for the start of fasting during the month of Ramadan. "Eat and drink until the moment when you will be able to distinguish the white thread from the black one. From this moment you have to strictly respect fasting until the night" (2:187).

Limited sexual contacts are present in Nazarene traditions. Most other Christians adopted this Nazarene tradition when marriage was forbidden during the days of Lent. Nevertheless, this prohibition on sexual conduct disappeared by the time of the Qur'an's revelation. "It is permitted to you to approach your wives on the night of the fasts" (2:187). However, it is still prohibited inside mosques: "Do not associate with your wives when you are in retreat in the mosques" (2:187).

Prayers

Prayer times are the same in Nazarene practices as they are in Islam. One is required to pray three times each day: in the morning, in the mid-day and in the evening. Outside these moments, prayer becomes optional. The very earliest non-canonical Christian text, "The Didache," orders, "We have to pray three times per day."[18] Hippolytus states that the Apostles taught, "The evening prayer is not compulsory,"[19] as did the Qur'an, "By night, it would be for you a supererogatory work" (17:79).

One finds further Qur'anic details. "O believers! Three occasions per day: Morning Prayer, the hour while you doff your clothes for the noonday heat; and after the late-night prayer" (24:58). In another verse, it calls for the mid-day prayer, "that of the middle" (2:238).

Regarding the direction of prayer, al-Qibla (the heavens' point) to which one has to turn for praying is "the sacred oratory" (Bayt al-Maqdis) in Nazarene polity,[20] as well as in the Qur'an. However, following the extreme tensions between Muhammad and Jews in Medina, the Sacred Oratory direction is removed from Jerusalem to Mecca (2:142, 145).

Women, Marriage and Divorce

Regarding women, marriage and divorce conditions one finds the similarity is the closest between Nazarenes and the Qur'an, as it was earlier between Jews and the Nazarenes.

According to the Jewish Talmud, "the maid's birth is a distress for the father."[21] The Qur'an does not waver much from this position. It states, "When news is brought to one of them, of the birth of a female child, his face darkens, and he is filled inner grief. With shame does he hide himself from his people, because of the bad news he has had" (16:58,59).

For Nazarenes, "public life is reserved to men, and it is convenient for women to stay at home and to live a life of restraint."[22] A mother speaks to her daughter: "I was a virgin maid and I did never go beyond the doorsteps of my parents' home."[23]

The Qur'an chides the prophet's wives: "Stay quietly in your houses and make not a dazzling display, like that of the former days of ignorance (al-Jahiliyyah)" (33:33).

Admonition to women

"Say to the believing women that they should lower their gaze and guard their modesty, that they should not display their beauty and ornaments except what must ordinarily appear thereof; that they should draw their veils over their bosoms and not display their beauty except to their husbands, their fathers, their husband's fathers, their sons, their husbands' sons, their brothers or their brothers' sons, or their sisters' sons or their women, or the slaves whom their right hands possess, or male servants free of physical needs for women" (24:31).

Jewish women faced nearly identical treatment. The Talmud explains, "If she bares her head in the street, walks quickly, talks to the passer-by, curses her husband's children, roars loudly, ... she will be repudiated."[24]

Divorce is an exclusive right for men.[25] Yet divorce remains an odious thing which God hates. (Malachi 2:16). The Talmud limits a man to four marriages.[26] Divorce is also an exclusive right inherent to the male according to several Suras (2:226-232,236-241; 4:128-130; 33:4,49). It is however still abominable. A couple of Hadith compilers state, "Divorce is the legal thing the most abominable for God."[27] The Qur'an stipulates, "the righteous marriage is with four women" (4:3).

Eucharist and Priesthood

Holy communion or Eucharist celebrations in sectarian, as well as Orthodox Christianity, produced many controversies. Certain texts prescribe it while others ignore the topic or speak about it with ambiguity.[28] The saintly Epiphanius notes that Ebionists celebrate their

Eucharist service with bread (al-fatir) and water instead of wine. This feast took place once a year at the same time, much like the Jewish Passover. Its worshipful purposes were for remembering and not innovative.[29] It was purely and simply a spiritual meal around which the faithful met with little discussion about offering thanks.

The Qur'an's position is not clear in this context. There is neither prescription nor proscription regarding its use. Sura five (The Table, al-ma'idah) shows Jesus with his disciples asking for "a table from heaven" (5:114). The disciples ask Jesus, son of Mary, to request God for this table (5:112), so that their hearts will be satisfied (5:113) with "a spread feast for the first and the last" (5:114). God hears this prayer (5:115). Jesus threatens those who do not believe with an unprecedented harsh penalty. "I will send it down unto you: but if any of you resisteth faith after this miracle, I will punish him with a penalty such as I have not inflicted on any one among all the peoples" (5:118). In a comment on this announcement, Denise Masson points out, "It is fitting to note that this form of words, particularly solemn, is appearing only this time in the Qur'an. God himself pronounces it."[30]

The ambiguous position regarding the importance of the Eucharist is linked to the question of a permanent priesthood. Indeed, neither Islam nor Nosrania finds a place for the Eucharist or a Priesthood. The Nazarenes believe that Jesus Christ was coming to abolish the offerings of Old Testament, which have been accomplished in conformity with the teaching of Moses.

The prophecy of Amos is typical of the biblical writers who complain about the ineffective priestly functions in the kingdom of Israel. "I hate, I despise your feasts, and I take no delight in your solemn assemblies... I, the Lord, will not look on your (Temple) offerings" (Amos 5:21). Psalm 50 states, "You will never take pleasure in sacrifice... What I want from you is your true thanks" (Psalm 50:14). Psalm 49 reads, "For a soul is far too precious to be ransomed by mere earthy wealth" (Psalm 49:8).

The Ebionists' teachings resonate with the message about the end of the official priesthood. "Through his baptism, the Messiah has blown out the fire kindled by the priest for sins' remission. So at a given time, sacrifice was necessary and essential, as well as a priesthood."[31] Subsequently, God abolishes the priestly functions of presiding over sacrifices and offerings and cancels the entire sacrificial system established for remission of sins.

Baptism, Divine Anointments

There is a single reference to baptism *(sibghah)* in the Qur'an. "It is a baptism from God; and who can be more able than God to provide this baptism?" (2:138). Normally, a priestly class introduces the novices into the faith within the Christian churches. Now this initiation rite is a work of God without the necessity of priests. In Arabia, there are ruins of churches where one finds a stone called "the black stone." It has been darkened by water that Azraqi refers to as baptismal founts where the water symbolized Christ.[32]

"This stone is the Christ." It is designated the "sweated stone" which leads to "bursts of water to quench thirsts, to cure ills, and purify sins."[33]

There are some archaeological traces of other black stones found in this central Arabia region. No one should be surprised to see the stones in ruins of baptismal founts that were once used for ritual purification and baptisms. The tantalizing question here is about the famous black stone in the center of the holy place in Mecca. Could that stone once have served as a baptismal fount? We know that in pre-Islamic times the Ka'ba had numerous biblical images. Abraham and the infant Jesus with Mary, his mother, were prominent. We also know that there were processions seven times around this Ka'ba, much like there were similar processions around churches and their baptisteries in pre-Islamic times.[34]

While the Qur'an is relatively silent about baptisms and priesthood, it does consider sacrifice as an act devoted to sins' remission. It clearly dismisses the priesthood as necessary for celebrating Holy Communion and baptism, however. The key to understanding the Qur'an's attitude toward priests may be tied to the use of the term "baptism or anointing" with which the faithful are initiated into faith. Let us look again at the word *sibghah*. "It is a baptism from God; and who can be more able than God to provide this baptism/anointing?" (2:138).

Who knows what is involved in the divine initiation mentioned only here in the Qur'an? Is there no divine unction available to Muhammad that would help him designate a successor as he comes to the close of his life in the Christian year 632?

If the objective of Waraqa was, as it was previously said, to find someone able to complete his mission in the Meccan church, his choice of Muhammad was providential. However, Muhammad was not able to look for his own successor as difficult conditions prevailed, involving new and more dangerous responsibilities such as the violence of his jihad, the insurrections of the Jews, and the phenomenal expansion of his mission from his initial calling in Mecca. All of these show how Muhammad changed from a transmitter and a warner into a messenger and a prophet and then to be the commander of the faithful.

Here lies the reason which prevented him from choosing a successor in the midst of mounting discords between Meccan immigrants and Medina supporters on one hand and on the other disputes with 'Ali's followers and the Arabs who would not stray from the security within Muhammad's family (Ahl al-Bayt). After Waraqa, there was the Prophet. Yet none would be anointed after Muhammad.

Chapter X

The Qur'an's Reflections of the Gospel Parables

The case has been made that the Nosrania priest, Waraqa Ibn Nawfal, introduced his cousin, Muhammad, to the Gospel. While there are no direct quotations from the biblical sources, the Qur'an borrows heavily from the earlier Scriptures. But this borrowing, which actually preserves a missing text called "The Gospel of the Hebrews," cannot be considered literary plagiarizing in the modern sense of the word.

The earlier revelations and their local environments are foundational to the study of biblical knowledge. This raises significant questions of why this kind of local environmental setting is missing when one looks at Muhammad's messages that take little or very little time in describing their lives' settings. This is especially lacking when it comes to introducing a particular biblical or non-biblical character. It is obvious that men like Moses, Noah, David and most other Old Testament persons are already known by the original listeners of the Qur'an and do not have to be re-introduced.

The parables of the Synoptic Gospels of Matthew, Mark and Luke often are portrayed in a setting that Jesus employs to introduce his main message. The Qur'an does follow this pattern in a few cases but more often it repeats the main message without a reference to its environmental setting.

Both Scriptures have a high view of their intrinsic truth. These views are proclaimed throughout their respective books and make no apologies for setting the bar for truth for themselves and for all times. The nature of revelation is something determined by the divine mind far beyond human culpability.

The Muslim holy book declares:

"God has set a seal on their hearts and on their hearing, and on their eyes is a veil; great is the penalty they incur... Fain would they deceive God and those who believe, but they only deceive themselves and realize it not! In their hearts is a disease, and God has increased their disease: grievous is the penalty they incur... They are the fools, but they do not know... God will throw back their mockery on them, and give them rope in their trespasses; so they will wander like blind ones, to and fro... Deaf, dumb, and blind, they will not return to the path... They press their fingers in their ears... If God will, he could take away their faculty of hearing and seeing" (2:7-20).

A similar view of itself is presented in the Christian and Hebrew Scriptures. "They look but do not see; they hear but don't listen nor understand... You will hear well, but not understand; you will do well, but don't see; for their hearts are fat and heavy, and their ears are dull, and they have closed their eyes in sleep, so they won't see and hear and understand; but turn to God again, and let me heal them" (Matthew 13:13; Mark 4:10-12; Luke 8:9-10; Romans 11:8; Isaiah 6:8-10, 29:10; Acts 28:26,27; Deuteronomy 29:4; John 12:40).

The Qur'an states that its acceptance by non-believers is related to the "doing of good" in words that are parallel to the Gospels' teaching about a godly man. From the Qur'an: "If we said: Enter this town and eat of the plenty therein as you wish, but enter the gate with humility, in posture and in words, and we shall forgive you your faults and increase the portion of those who do well" (2:58). From the Matthew Gospel: "Whenever you enter a city or a village, search for a godly man and stay in his home until you leave for the next town" (Matthew 10:13,14).

The two revelations that are the sources of faith for millions deal with lessons of basic morality. The Qur'an is filled with warnings regarding ethical behavior. "O believers! Do not say: 'Ra'ina'.. A grievous punishment is prepared for unbelievers" (2:104). A similar injunction is found in the Gospel.

"Whoever calls his brother 'idiot' is in danger of the fire of hell" (Matthew 5:22). "Do you enjoin right conduct on the people, and forget to practice it yourselves?" asks the Qur'an (2:44). This admonition may be read in the light of the Gospel of Matthew's remarks about hypocrisy.

"They load you with impossible demands that they themselves don't even try to keep" (Matthew 23:4).

The highest ethical standard that the Qur'an demands is the forsaking of all forms of idolatry. The Exodus (32:8) account of the Israelites worshipping the golden calf is cited in the second Sura, entitled The Calf, to memorialize the Old Testament event. "You have indeed wronged yourselves by your worship of the calf. So turn in repentance to your creator" (2:54). Self-sacrifice is perhaps the highest ethical standard coming from the mouth of Jesus. "For any one who keeps his life for himself shall lose it" (Matthew 16:25; Luke 9:24; Mark 8:35). Jesus himself set the highest and most unobtainable goal for a follower of Jesus. "Be perfect as your Father in heaven is perfect." The first step toward this goal is Jesus' advice to a rich man, "If you want to be perfect, go and sell everything you have" (Matthew 19:21).

The obvious differences between abandonment of idols and the abandonment of one's self are vast and deserve fuller exegetical study than what is proposed in this work. Hopefully any common words, structures and meanings, especially in the parables of the two texts, can help us understand major conformities and differences between the Qur'an and the Bible.

"Charity" or acts of goodwill is a good place to start this comparative study. The Qur'an warns, "God knows what every one of you spend in charity...If you disclose acts of charity, even so it is well, but if you conceal them, and make them reach those really in need, that is best for you: it will remove from you some of your stains of evil. God is well acquainted with what you do. Whatever good you give benefits your souls, and you shall only do so seeking the face of God. Whatever good you give, shall be rendered back to you, and shall not be dealt with unjustly. Who spends in charity of good by night and by day, in secret and in public, have their reward with their Lord: on them shall be no fear, nor shall they grieve." (2:270-274). "Call on your Lord with humility and in private" (7:55), says the Qur'an about private prayers.

Over seven centuries earlier than the Qur'anic revelation, Jesus speaks about public and private prayers, as well as deeds of charity. "When you pray, go into your room and shut the door and pray to your Father in secret" (Matthew 6:6). "Your father who knows every secret, will reward you" (Matthew 6:18). "Take care! Do not do your good deeds publicly, to be admired, for then you will lose the reward from your Father in heaven. When you give a gift to a beggar, don't shout about it as the hypocrites do, in order to call attention to their acts of charity and be rewarded... They have received all the reward they will ever get... When you do a kindness to someone, do it secretly.... Your Father who knows all secrets will reward you" (Matthew 6:1,2).

The phrase about a 'camel going through the eye of a needle' provides some precise words that appear in the two Scriptures. Both texts highlight the impossibility of the camel going through a small gate in the walls of Jerusalem. The subjects of this dilemma are those who are arrogant (Qur'anic listener) and those who are rich (Gospel listener). "To those who reject our signs and treat them with arrogance, no opening will there be of gates of heaven, nor will they enter the Paradise, until the camel can pass through the eye of the needle" (7:40). From the New Testament, "It is almost impossible for a rich person to get into the Kingdom of Heaven. I say it again: It is easier for a camel to go through the eye of a needle than for a rich man to enter the Kingdom of God" (Matthew 19:23,24).

Ethical Models

Forgiveness is an important concept in the two Scriptures. The Qur'an cries, "Our Lord! Condemn us not if we forget or fall into error. Our Lord! Lay not on us a burden like that which you did lay on those before us. Our Lord! Lay not on us a burden greater than we have strength to bear. Blot out our sins, and grant us forgiveness. Have mercy on us, Thou art our Lord; help us against those who stand against faith" (2:286). "Our Lord! Forgive us our faults, blot out from us our sins" (3:193). Jesus' instruction to his disciples includes the following prayer. "Our Father! ... Bring us not into temptation... Forgive us our sins just as we have forgiven those who have sinned against us" (Matthew 6:12-13). "Forgive our sins, as we have forgiven those who sinned against us. And do not allow us to be tempted" (Luke 11:4).

The Qur'an's own words against hypocrites who pray are very familiar to the Gospel. "When they stand up to pray, they stand without earnestness, to be seen of men" (4:142). "Woe to the worshippers who are neglectful of their prayers, those who want but to be seen of men" (107:4-6). The Matthew Gospel issues these words of Jesus, "When you pray, do not be like the hypocrites who pretend pity by praying publicly on street corners and in synagogues where everyone can see them" (Matthew 6:5).

Familial versis divine loyality are covered in the two texts. "If it be that your fathers, your sons, your brothers, your mates, or your children, the wealth that you have gained, are dearer to you than God, or his apostle, or the striving in his cause, then wait until God brings about his decision" (9:24). Love for Jesus, the Messiah, is far superior than love of family. "He who loves his father or his mother, his son or his daughter more than me, is not worthy of me (Matthew 10:37).

Numbers in the Two Texts

"If you ask seventy times for their forgiveness, God will not forgive them" (9:80).

"Forgive him not only seven times but even seventy times" (Matthew 18:21,22).

If three persons are together, he makes the fourth among them, nor between five but he makes the sixth, nor between fewer nor more, but he is in their midst, wheresoever they be" (58:7).

"For where two or three gather together because they are mine, I will be right there among them" (Matthew 18:20).

"Who will loan to God a beautiful loan, God will multiply it many times" (2:245) is the Qur'an's identification with the words of the Gospels. "For to him who has, will more be given" (Matthew 13:12; Luke 8:18; 19:26).

"Even if we did send unto them angels...they would not believe..."(6:111). This warning from the Qur'an is close to warnings that Jesus spoke to his listeners. "If they do not listen to Moses and the prophets, they won't listen even though someone rises from the dead" (Luke 16:31). Both the Qur'an and the Bible appeal to the great law-giver, Moses. The Qur'an rremarks, " But why they ask you to be their arbiter? Yet they have the Pentateuch, therein is the command of God" (5:43). "They have Moses and the prophets, they should listen to them" (Luke 16:29). Both texts return to the same conclusions regarding indifferent listeners. Jesus comments, "These people say they honor me, but their hearts are far away" (Matthew 15:8). The hypocrites who refuse to fight alongside of the Muslims in

Medina were described as "Saying with their lips what was not not in their hearts" (3:167).

The excuses for not following the path to truth are similar. "Among them is a man who says: 'Grant me exemption and draw me not into trial.' Have they not fallen into trial already?" (9:49). (According to an unattributable tradition, these were slackers who asked the prophet to allow them to be relieved from following him because they were loved of women.) Jesus had to deal with another excuse. "Another from his disciples said: Let me first say farewell to my family" (Luke 9:57-61; Matthew 8:19-22).

Reconciliation of Parties

Doing good to one another is central to the two records. The Qur'anic teaching on reconciliation is very close to the Matthew account. "If two parties among the believers fall into a quarrel, make you peace between them; but if one of them transgresses beyond bounds against the other, then all fight against the one that transgresses until he complies with the command of God," the Qur'an continues, "if he complies, then make peace between them with justice, and be fair..." Reconciliation is essential, "The believers are but a single brotherhood. So make peace and reconciliation between your two brothers; and fear God, that you may receive mercy..."(49:9,10).

The words of the Gospel are to the believer who has been wronged. "If your brother sins against you, go to him privately and confront him with his fault. If he listens and confesses it, you have won back a brother. But if not, then take one or two others with you and go back to him again, proving everything you say by these witnesses." Jesus continues, "If he still refuses to listen, then take your case to the church, and if the church's verdict favors you, but he will not accept it, then he should be considered as a pagan" (Matthew 18:15).

The correction of the behavior of a follower of the Gospel should be handled like family members. "Beware that you do not look down upon a single one of those little children" (Matthew 18:10). "If you are only angry with your brother, even in your own home, you are in danger of judgment! If you call your brother an idiot, you are in danger of being brought before the community" (Matthew 5:21). Likewise, the Qur'an warns against despising others with sarcasm and offensive nicknames. "Let not some men among you laugh at others; it may be that the latter are better than the former... Nor defame nor be sarcastic to each other, nor call each other by offensive nicknames, ill-seeming is a name connoting wickedness, after he has believed" (49:11).

Regarding the ethics of the Gospel and the Qur'an it appears that they are on parallel courses. The Qur'an is less precise in defining its community compared to the Gospel of Matthew on this topic. The community in the days of Muhammad and his cousin-priest, Waraqa, was already a well-defined community, the church in Mecca. The community at the time of Jesus was not highly developed. One thing is obvious; the Qur'an itself declares that much of its ethical standards were built on previous scriptural systems, as was the case when Jesus cited the Hebrew Scriptures. "I have come," Jesus explains in Matthew 5:17, "Not to abolish the law and the prophets but to fulfill them." Both texts use the literary device of parables in their teachings.

The Use of Parables

From the Qur'an: "What means God by this parable?" (2:26).

"God talks to the people with parables" (14:24).

"We put parables in your behalf" (14:45).

"God sets forth, for a parable to the unbelievers" (66:10).

From Matthew 13: "He spoke about a lot of items in parables" (13:3).

"That is why I used with them parables" (13:13).

"He used with them another parable" (13:24).

"Then he also used another parable" (13:33).

Among the best-known parables is the story of the seeds that were scattered on the ground by a Palestinian sower. In its original Gospel setting this Sower parable is based upon an everyday agricultural process that Jesus relates to the Kingdom of God. The Qur'an embellishes this story to talk about three successive religious and political systems.

The sower parable clearly reveals a setting when Islam was replacing the older faith systems of the Jews and Christians in seventh century Arabia. This would be the situation several years following the death of the prophet. "Look to what they are compared in the Pentateuch and the Gospel, like a seed which sends forth its blade; then makes it strong; it then becomes thick and it stands on its own stem, filling the sower with wonder and delight... God has promised forgiveness and a great reward to them who believe" (48:29).

Without this expanded account of the Parable of the Sower, the Qur'an uses the Sower parable to draw a conclusion that is different than that of Matthew 13. "The parable of those who spend their substance in the way of God is that of a grain of wheat; it grows seven ears, and each ear has a hundred grains. God gives manifold increase to whom he pleases." The Qur'anic parable is of those who spend their wealth in public to be seen of men. They are in the parable "like a hard barren rock, which has little soil... and the likeness of those who spend their substance seeking to please God...is a garden high and fertile; heavy rains fall on it but it yields a double increase of harvest" (2:261-265).

The Gospel parable simply states, "Here is the parable of the sower who was sowing wheat in his fields. As he scattered the seed across the ground, some fell on rocky soil. The hot sun scorched them and they withered and died. But some fell on good soil and produced a crop that was thirty, sixty and even a hundred times as much as he had planted" (Matthew 13:5-8; Luke 8:6-8).

The Qur'an mixes other teachings of the Gospel into its pages. Its Arabic version of the Sower mentions those "who spend their substance to be seen by men" (2:264) which is material from Matthew 6:1 which says, "Beware of practicing your piety before men in order to be seen by them."

Lazarus and Abraham

Another example of the Qur'an's borrowing and reinterpreting of an earlier Gospel story is the parable of the rich man and the beggar Lazarus. The New Testament story comes from Jesus' teaching in Luke (16:19-26). The Qur'an provides some new forms to draw different lessons from the original Lukan account which is cast in midst of the Qur'an's teaching about the separation of the righteous from the evil ones without mentioning Lazarus and Abraham (18:39-44; 7:42-48). The Lukan text is a dialogue that takes place between the poor man Lazarus and a rich man through Abraham, the patriarch. This rich man is splendidly clothed and lives each day in luxury. One day, Lazarus, the beggar, dies and is carried to Abraham's bosom. The rich man also dies, and his soul goes to Hades. There in constant torment, he sees Lazarus from a distance with Abraham.

"Father Abraham," he shouts, "have some pity! Send Lazarus here if only to dip the tip of his finger in water and cool my tongue, for I am in anguish in these flames."

The gospel narrative goes on, "Son, remember that during your lifetime you had everything you wanted and Lazarus had nothing. Now he is here being comforted and you are in anguish..." (Luke 16:24,25).

In the Qur'an the dialogue takes place between the inhabitants of paradise and those of fire through the men of al-A'raf that will be reviewed in Chapter XI.

The parable of the wise man who builds his house on solid rock is referenced in the Qur'an (9:109) where it asks, "Which is better? He who lays his foundation on piety to Allah or he that lays his foundation on a weak sandy cliff ready to crumble to pieces?" The Qur'an continues with a description of Hell. The story that Jesus tells keeps the narrative simple and allows the listener to interpret any eschatological implication that could arise from this moral story. "Though the rain comes in torrents... and the storm winds beat against his house, it will not collapse, for it is built on rock. And everyone who hears these words of mine and does not do them will be like the foolish man who builds his house on sand, for when the rains and floods come, and storm winds beat against his house, it will fall with a mighty crash" (Matthew 7:24-27).

The parable of a fruitful tree and an unfruitful tree mingle in the Qur'an with the parable of the mustard seed in the following manner: "Do you not see how God sets forth a parable? A godly word is like a godly tree whose root is firmly fixed and its branches reach to the heavens... And the parable of an evil word is that of an evil tree: it is ripped out by the root from the ground because it has no stability. God will establish in strength those who believe in this word and in the hereafter" (14:24-27).

The Qur'anic parable is adopted from the Gospel of Matthew (13:31,32): "The tiny mustard seed is the smallest seed planted in a field but becomes the largest of the plants, and grows into a big tree." The fruitful tree metaphors of the Qur'an come also from this Gospel source. "Different kinds of fruit trees can quickly be identified by examining their fruit. A variety that produces delicious fruit never produces an inedible kind. And a tree producing an inedible kind will not produce what is good. So the trees having inedible fruit are chopped down..." (Matthew 7:17-19). "A tree from good stock does not produce scrub fruit nor do trees from poor stock produce choice fruit. A tree is identified by the kind of fruit it produces. It is like a good man producing good deeds from a good heart" (Luke 4:43).

One can trace the earlier Gospel parable embedded in the Qur'an's account of a faithful servant and an evil servant. "God sets forth the parable of two men: one a slave under the dominion of another. He has no power of any sort. And the other a man on whom we have bestowed many good favors. He spends thereof free, privately and publicly: Are the two equal?" (16:75). The Matthew Gospel speaks of the disparity of the two servants that begins with a question. "Who is then the wise and faithful servant of the Lord? The one who managed well his household... or that one who began partying and getting drunk?" (Matthew 24:45-51).

Finally, the parable of the ten bridesmaids that is only mentioned in Matthew's Gospel appears in the Qur'an with significant differences. The major dialogue between wise and foolish women of the Gospel is presented in the Qur'an between hypocritical men and women on one side, and believing men and women on the other. The hypocrites ask the believers to give them oil for their light. The believers answer by telling the foolish ones to return back and buy oil for their lamps. When they leave, the gate is closed behind them. The hypocrites are locked out and beg the believers to open the gate for them, but there was nobody to hear.

"One day shall you see the believing men and women, how their light runs forward before them and by their right hands: Their greeting will be: Good News for you this day! Gardens beneath which flow rivers to dwell therein forever! ... One day will the hypocrites - men and women - say to the believers: 'Wait for us! Let us borrow a light from your light!' It will be said: "Turn back to your rear! Then seek a light!' So a wall will be put up between them with a gate therein... Those without will call out: 'Were we not with you?' The others will reply: 'True, but you led yourselves into temptation; you looked forward to our ruin; you doubted God's promise; and your false desires deceived you! ... And the deceiver deceived you...!'" (57:12-14). The Matthew account indirectly applies divine judgment at the conclusion of the parable, which becomes more apparent in the language of an end times "wedding feast."

"Ten bridesmaids took their lamps and went to meet the bridegroom, but only five were wise enough to fill their lamps with oil, while the other five were foolish and forgot.... At midnight, the five who had not any oil begged the others to share with them, for their lamps were going out. But others replied: 'we have not enough. Go instead to the shops and buy some for yourselves!' But while they were gone, the bridegroom came, and those who were ready went in with him to the marriage feast, and the door was locked. Later, when the other five returned, they stood outside, calling: 'Sir, open the door for us!' But he called back: 'Go away! It is too late!'... There shall be weeping and gnashing of teeth." (Matthew 25:1-13).

The parables selected for this chapter help the reader understand the cultural and social life of Jesus and his first century contemporaries. The Qur'an does not hesitate to recognize that it has borrowed heavily from the earlier scriptures and with that textual borrowing comes a great deal about the milieu of the first century. There is far less known about the Muslim first century at the time that the Qur'an was proposed as "an easy commentary of the foreign book" (41:44; 73:20). There is no identification of this foreign book and how it became the predecessor to the Qur'an. The lack of a historical perspective is due largely to the high sense of revelation that Muslims attach to the Qur'an. It places the Qur'an far beyond any mortal's capability of understanding because this holy book belongs to the highest point in heaven and not to any one human culture.

Taha Hussein, an eminent Egyptian writer, expressed in the last century what has always been a highly unpopular opinion for all of the fourteen centuries of Islamic existence. He asks his fellow Muslims to think about the Jews at the time of Muhammad. Hussein states, "It is not easy at all to understand the opposition that these rabbis held against the Qur'an because they had no links to it."[1] The Jews discussed and ended up rejecting the prophet and the book without having understood its mysteries and realities. Hussein goes on to conclude, "It seems also more difficult and even impossible to believe that the Qur'an was completely new for the Arabs. They would neither grasp nor deeply understand its objective, nor believe in its message."[2]

One should be able to recognize, as well as to honor, Waraqa who translated the Gospel to the Hebrews for the Arabs and explained it to Muhammad during the forty-four years they served together in Mecca.

Chapter XI

The Hereafter - Hell

The Qur'an, the Pentateuch, and the Talmud, as well as the Gospels, use a number of words and expressions to designate hell or Gehenna. The word hell is repeated over seventy times in the Qur'an. From a linguistic point of view, this Hebrew word comes from "the Valley of Bin Hinnom" (Joshua 18:16; Jeremiah 32:35). In Old Testament times the temple of the deity Molk was erected there and was the place where pagans cremated their human victims. This small area near the walls of Jerusalem became the valley in which "dead human bodies will be food for birds and animals of the earth" according to the prophecy of Jeremiah (7:31-33). "The dead bodies of those who have rebelled against me. For their worm shall never die, their fire shall not be quenched" (Isaiah 66:24).

Regarding the word Gehenna it has another meaning as an underground dwelling place for the dead. According to Jewish traditions, darkness, fire and torments dominate in this infernal place.[1] New Testament uses of the word are based upon the earlier texts (Matthew 5:22,29,30; 10:28; 18:9; 23:15). The Jewish Talmud locates Gehenna in the earth's center[2] with seven parts.[3] Its size is unlimited.[4] It dips in full darkness.[5] Its fire is sixty times more blazing than that of the earth.[6]

Other synonyms for this term are found in the Qur'an: jahim (twenty-six times), sa'ir (sixteen times), and naar, fire (more than a hundred times) being the most frequent. Among the less used terms are saqr (four times), al-Hutamah (104: 4,5) which translates as "that which smashes or breaks to pieces," al-laza (70:15) or the fire of the hell, "the penalty of the burning fire" (85:10), "the pit of blazing fire" (101:9-11), and "the precipice of fire" (3:103).

All these Qur'anic expressions have cognates in the Pentateuch and the Talmud, where hell means ditch, precipice or al-Tahom, that indicates the rising sea from which the flood comes (Genesis 8: 20); and tophet (deep and wide ditch) "where it is piled high with fire and wood. The breath of the Lord, like fire of the volcano, will set it on fire" (Isaiah 30:33).

The fact that the Qur'an qualifies hell as a "an foreboding place to rest in" (14:29), "an evil plight" (25: 34) and "a place of decrepitude" (14:28) allows for the comparison of these terms with biblical descriptions, as "the dwelling from which the man can never escape" (Job 7:9). The graphic descriptions of hell have been defended by the Church Fathers, like Hippolytus of Rome,[7] Ignatius of Antioch,[8] and Cyril of Jerusalem.[9]

Physical Descriptions of Hell

The Qur'anic hell has seven grades in conformity with "seven gates" (15:44). Al-Jalalayn explains them as being seven steps. Angels watch over these gates to allow the inmates to enter. The angels beckon through the open gate. "Go in through the gates of Gehenna, you will stay therein forever" (16:29; 39:71,72).

According to Jewish sources hell has seven grades,[10] but only three gates. "The first is from the desert, the second from the sea and the third from Jerusalem."[11] Job speaks about "the gates of Death" or "the gates of death's shadow" (38:17) while Isaiah gives more details about "the gates of Sheol" (38:10).

Sins leading the condemned to hell are numberless. The Qur'an mentions many sins beginning with scriptural desecrations. "Those who conceal the clear signs we have sent down, and the guidance, ...on them shall be God's curse" (2:159). "Those who break God's covenant after it is ratified are lost only to themselves" (2:27). The Lord will curse those who falsify and corrupt God's words or change something in the revealed books. "A party of them heard the word of God, and perverted it knowingly after they understood it" (2:75). "Woe to those who write the book with their own hands... Woe to them, for what their hands do write" (2:79). "There is among them a section who distort the book with their tongue: as they read you would think it is a part of the book" (3:78). "There are among Jews those who displace words from their right places, ... God has cursed them" (4:46). "We cursed them, the Nasrania, for they change the words from their right places" (5:14).

The final book in the New Testament has this warning "Everyone who reads the prophetic words in this book and adds anything to what is written here, God shall increase to him the plagues... And if anyone subtracts any part of these prophecies, God shall take away his share in the tree of life and in the holy city described in this book" (Revelation 22:18,19).

Additional curses are found in both Meccan and Medinan sections of the Qur'an. "Those who annoy God and his apostle, will be cursed by God in this world and in the hereafter" (33:57); "Those who invent a lie against God, the curse of God is on those who do wrong; those who would hinder men from the path of God, these are impious" (11:18,19). "Those who break the covenant of God, and work mischief on the earth, on them is the curse; for them is the terrible home!" (13:25). "He who kills a believer intentionally, his recompense is hell, to abide therein forever" (4:93).

Qur'anic Images of the Damned

"So, by the Lord, without doubt, we shall gather them together, and the evils with them; then we shall bring them forth on their knees round about hell.

Then we shall certainly drag out from every sect all those who were worst in obstinate rebellion against God most gracious.

And certainly we know best those who are most worthy of being burned therein.

There will no one of you to pass over it; this is a decree taken by your Lord.

Then we shall save those who fear, and we shall leave the wrongdoers therein humbled to their knees" (19:68-72).

The Qur'an comments on the large number of condemned at the entry to hell who are divided into groups. "We shall drive the sinners to hell like thirsty cattle driven to water" (19:86). "The unbelievers will be led to hell in crowd" (39:71). Hell is filled with men and Jinns... " but my word is true: I will fill hell with Jinns and men together" (32:13). Hell will be gorged, for its size is boundless. "One day we will ask hell: Art thou filled to the full? It will reply: Are there more to come?" (50:30).

The Pentateuch and the Gospels evoke similar remarks. The poet-prophet Isaiah said: "Sheol is licking its chops in anticipation of this delicious morsel, her great and small shall be swallowed" (Isaiah 5:14). The Book of Proverbs strikes another poetic line: "There are three things never satisfied: hell (sheol), the barren womb and the desert" (Proverbs. 30:15,16).

Matthew's Gospel highlights the broadness of the road leading to hell and at the easy access to it. "The highway to hell is broad and is gate is wide enough for all the multitudes who choose its easy way. But the gateway to life is small and the road is narrow, and only a few ever find it" (Matthew 7:13,14).

The Question of Hell's Eternity

Two divergent opinions arise from the Qur'an regarding torments of hell. Are these torments eternal or provisional? The texts which support the ideas for eternal torment are as follows:

"Any that disobey God and his apostle, will have the fire of Gehenna as a reward, and shall dwell therein forever" (72:23). "Verily God has cursed the unbelievers and prepared for them a blazing fire to dwell therein forever" (33:64,65). "The people of fire will dwell therein forever" (2:39).

The second position refers to Qur'anic texts that designate provisionary punishment. "They will dwell therein for all the time that the heavens and the earth endure, except as your Lord is the sure Perfector of what he plans" (11:106-108). "The fire be your dwelling-place; you will dwell therein forever, except as God wills. For he is full of wisdom and knowledge" (6:128).

The question of whether there is an eternal or shorter duration in hell belongs to the judgment of God, to his freewill and to his absolute power. "For God will do what he likes" (22:14). "God does command according to his will and plan" (5:1). "He is Doer of all that he intends" (85:16; 11:107).

When the Qur'an recognizes the temporary torments, it comes close to the Christian, at least in the Nosrania tradition of the possible existence of a purgatory. This in-between state following death provides a place where humans can atone for sins before gaining entrance to paradise. From the early days of Muhammad's mission some Muslims have debated this issue. Contemporaries of Muhammad attribute to him a hadith in which he would say: "People of paradise will stay there and those of the fire in fire." He would also say: "Let go this attitude of having in one's heart a creed equivalent to the weight of a grain of mustard seed. He will be brought out after having been darkened [by the smoke of hell], and led to the river of life." [12]

One finds in Christianity a similar orientation. Origen's summary on this subject is from his famous treatise called "Comprehensive Restoration",[13] according to some texts drawn from the Gospels and the Acts.[14]

The veil of al-A'raf, described in the Qur'an, deals with a state between heaven and hell.

"Between them shall be a veil, and on the heights (al-A'raf, Sura 7) will be men who would know every one by his marks: they will call out to the companions of the paradise: Peace on you. They will not have entered, but they will have an assurance thereof. And when their eyes shall be turned towards the companions of the fire, they will say:

O Lord, Send us not to the company of the wrongdoers. The men on the heights will call to certain men whom they will know from their marks, saying: Of what profit to you were your hoards and your arrogant ways?" (7:46-48).

It appears that the veil of al-A'raf is the high wall separating paradise from hell. People of al-A'raf walk on this high wall which is also "the way to the Fire" (37:23), or the bridge over which men should cross after death. The pre-Islamic religion of Persia often identified as Mazdean refers to this bridge as Sinfat. It would be at the gate of hell. Jewish and Nosrania, as well as other Christian sects, mention it. "It is a narrow road over a ditch."[15]

People of al-A'raf have no particular sign of distinction. Nothing will indicate if their destiny is the heavens or hell which means that they are between both since they walk on the high wall. They have not reached their ultimate destination. Their identity is not established. But they know well the people of paradise, as well as those of hell. They warn the people from crossing the high road without light.

"One day will the hypocrites - men and women - say to the believers: Wait for us! Let us borrow a light from your light. It will be said: Turn you back to your rear! Then seek a light! So a wall be put up between them with a gate herein" (57:13). The parables of the Ten

Virgin Bridesmaids (Matthew 25:1-13 and Lazarus and the rich man (Luke 16:19-26) form the background of Sura 57.

The damned in hell will not be able to make distinctions between life and death. "He who comes to his Lord as a sinner, for him is hell: herein shall he neither die nor live" (20:74), but he will die twice. "Our Lord! Twice hast Thou made us without life, and twice hast Thou given us life! Now have we recognized our sins: is there any way out of this?" (40:11). In the Qur'an, as in the Book of Revelation, there is a statement about those who are delivered from final death. "Nor will they there taste death, except the first death" (44:56). "There is nothing beyond our first death" (44:35). The Qur'an inquires, "Shall we match other penalties of a similar kind? Shall we burn in the fire?" (37:58,59). And from Revelation (2:11), "He who is victorious shall not be hurt by the second death." "The lake of fire is the second death" (Revelation 20:14).

Fire and Darkness

The servere punishments of the damned in hell is multidimensional-physical as well as psychological. According to the Qu'ran fires cover the inmates from all sides. "Hell will encompass the rejecters of faith... On the day the punishment shall cover them from above them and from below them" (29:54,55). The fire will go out and cover their hearts. "It is the fire of God kindled to a blaze, which does mount right to the hearts. It shall be made into a vault over them, in columns outstretched" (104:6-9). They will sleep on fire and will be covered with fire. "For them there is Gehenna as a couch below and fire of covering above" (7:41).

As far as the Christian and Nosrania traditions, one finds lucid images of the eternal fires built upon Jewish traditions. The apocryphal book of Enoch says, "Darkness will be their dwelling. Worms will be in their bed. They will never have hope to go out thereof."[16] According to the Qur'an, "the companions of the left hand will be in the midst of a fierce blast of fire and in boiling water and in the shades of black smoke" (56:42,43). The fourth century monk, Ephrem the Syrian, uses the Syriac language to convey an early Orthodox theology of the hereafter. He expresses his vivid thoughts in biblical and extra-biblical metaphors. "The damned will be in the lake of fire. They will suffer without any hope to go out thereof. The blaze of fire will cover them from all sides.[17] Their mouth will even vomit fire." Ephrem adds in another work: "The damned in Gehenna will eat fire."[18]

The Gospels freely recall the descriptive words of Jesus warning his listeners about the coming fires. The damned are huddled in deep darkness covering them from any help (Matthew 8:12). In the eschatological message Jesus delivers to his disciples about dividing the sheep from the goats, he states that eternal fire is "prepared for the devil and his angels" (Matthew 25:41). The rebellious angels of hell "will be kept in eternal chains in the nether gloom until the great day of judgment" (Jude 6). The question of fire with darkness is resolved in the Enoch book. "The light will disappear before them, and their dwelling will be covered by darkness forever."[19]

The Qur'an's message to the Arabs of both Mecca and Medina continues the strong, threatening words. "Fear the fire whose fuel is men and stones, which is prepared for those who reject faith" (2:24). "As to those who are rebellious and wicked, their abode will be the fire. Every time they wish to get away, they will be forced thereunto, and it will be said to them: Taste you the penalty of the fire" (32:20). "Pour over their heads the penalty of boiling water" (44:48). "Fire will cover their faces" (14:49,50). "Those who told lies against God, their faces will be turned black" (39:60), as if they were a part of a dark night. The Qur'an states, "Their faces will be covered, as it were, with pieces from the depths of the darkness of night" (10:27). "Other faces will be dust-stained. Blackness will cover them" (80:40,41). "Some faces, that day, will be sad and dismal" (75:24).

Concerning the pathos of the ones condemned, the Qur'an imagines their cries that will be indescribable because of pain and humiliation. "There, sobbing will be their lot, nor will they hear nothing else" (21:100). The fire of hell is for those who oppose God and his apostle, wherein they shall dwell, that is the supreme disgrace" (9:63). "You will see them brought forward to the penalty in a humble frame of mind because of their disgrace and looking with a stealthy glance" (42:45). "Those who are wretched shall be in the fire: there will be for them therein nothing but the heaving of sighs and sobs" (11:106).

In the Gospels, the sounds of the damned are not any better than that described in the Qur'an. Those condemned will be in "outer darkness where men will weep and gnash their teeth" (Matthew 8:12). The Matthew gospel repeats this phrase on five other occasions

(13:42,50; 22:13; 24:51; 25:30). Their remorse and their contrition will not be heard, as is the case of the rich man who suffers the punishments in the hell. He will ask Abraham to intercede in his favor, but Abraham would not be able to offer help (Luke 16:19-26).

Among the awful torments of hell and described by the Qur'an is the fastening of the bodies of the damned in collars, chains and handcuffs. "We have put yokes round their necks, right up to their chins, so that their heads are forced up and they cannot see" (36:8). "The yokes shall be round their necks and the chains shall be dragged along" (40:71). "We have prepared for the rejecters of faith chains, yokes and a blazing fire" (76:4). "We have fetters to bind them and a fire to burn them" (73:12).

Food and Drink in Hell

"Verily the tree of Zaqquman, will be the food of the sinful, like molten brass; it will boil their insides, like the boiling of scalding water" (44:43-46). "For it is a tree that springs out of the bottom of hell-fire. The shoots of its fruit-stalks are like the heads of devils" (37:63-68). "It is a cursed tree" (17:60). "No food will there be for them but bitter Dhari which neither nourishes nor satisfies hunger" (88:6,7). "It is a food that chokes, and a penalty grievous" (73:13). "They swallow into themselves naught but fire" (2:174).

"Those who reject God will have draughts of boiling fluids" (10:4), "a drink that chokes the insides" (47:15). "Nothing cool shall they taste therein, nor any drink, save a boiling fluid, and a fluid dark, murky, intensely cold, a fitting recompense" (78:25,26). "Frustration is the lot of every powerful obstinate transgressor, in front of such a one is hell, and he is given, for drink, boiling fetid water" (14:16,17)

In the Qur'an, chapter 88, there is a summary of food and drinks reserved for the damned.

Some faces, that day, will be humiliated,
Laboring hard and weary, burning in blazing fire,
They are given to drink of a boiling hot spring,
No food will there be for them but a bitter Dhari,
that will neither nourish nor satisfy hunger. (88:2-7)

Angels accompanying death

The apocryphal book of Enoch, the preChristian author reports, "chains of iron and bars which bear the angels in charge to execute the torments."[20] It is analogous to Matthew's Gospel: "The king said to his aids: Bind him hand and foot and throw him out into the outer darkness" (Matthew 22:13). Other Christian writers note angelic activity: "The wrath of God binds the damned to a column, the angels come down bearing bars and chains..."[21]

The angels of hell play a role in the death and the damnation of the transgressors. Here the status as supernatural beings s not unlike some of Nazarene and other Christian literature like that which is found in Islamic traditions. The Qur'an talks about the angel of death. "Say: the Angel of Death, put in charge of you, will duly take your souls, then shall you be brought back to your Lord" (32:11). In Muslim tradition his name is 'Izra'il who takes the souls of people following their death. The death angel who divides a dead person in two parts has no power over believers among Jews who keep well the Pentateuch.[22]

The procedure at death happens in the following manner: "When the human being leaves this world, then the angel of death appears to bring out his soul. If he is innocent, his soul will be taken out smoothly, as a hair taken out from a cup of milk. But if he was sinful, his soul will be wretched from his body like pressed water springing from a narrow trough."[23]

The Qur'an describes this phenomenon: "Those who tear out (the souls of the wicked) with violence, and those who gently draw out (the souls of the blessed)" (79:1,2). Al-Jalalayn contrasts the two actions, "angels who tear out the souls of bad people with fierceness and those who smoothly take out the souls of good people."[24]

When the angel of death achieves his task, two other angels will approach the dead. They are Harout and Marout (2:102). One will stay on the right and the other on the left. Each one will conduct him on the way he merits. "Behold, two guardian angels, appointed to receive the dead, one sitting on the right, and one on the left" (50:17). If the dead belongs to the damned, God will send him two other angels: "one to carry him and another to bear witness" (50:21) before throwing him into fire. "Throw into hell every contentious rejecter of God... Throw him into a severe penalty" (50:24).

When these two angels arrive with the dead before the gates of hell, the deceased will be taken by nineteen bad angels who "smite their faces and their backs" (47:27). They are called Zabaniyah, or angels of punishment," angels stern and severe" (66:6), "guardians of fire" (74:26-31) and hell keepers. "Every time a group (of unbelievers) is cast therein, its keepers will ask: 'Did no warner come to you?'" (67:8). The name Zabaniyah is possibly related to the Syriac term Shabayah employed by Ephrem to describe the fierce angels "who rush down the damned into hell."[25]

Jewish and Christian traditions and legends follow a wide spectrum of ideas when it comes to the subject of angels in the Hereafter. The good angels will bear the innocents to paradise while the bad will deal with torments to be inflicted on the damned. "The Lord dispatches against them a band of destroying angels" (Psalm 78:49).

The Pentateuch recalls the two angels who intercede for Lot. "For we will destroy the city completely. Jehovah has sent us to destroy it" (Genesis 19:1-13). In his apocryphal book, Enoch says: "I saw some lines of malicious angels bearing in their hands bars and chains of iron and copper superheated in order to torture the damned."[26]

These angels are, writes St. Pachome, fierce and unmerciful. "God has created them, devoid of mercy, so they do not evince any compassion towards the damned."[27]

Briefly, instructions concerning the Last Day, Resurrection, Paradise and Hell are foremost teachings of Muhammad. While in Mecca the subject of doom and heaven and hell became the main items of his preaching. His eschatological descriptions, agree widely with what was part of the creed of the Nosrania church in his hometown.[28] The more one pursues thoroughly into this research, one will discover the significant connections between al-Qiss Waraqa and his student's teaching and preaching on the subjects that are found in this chapter and that will continue in the following chapter.

Chapter XII

Coming Last Day and Paradise

Qur'anic and Christian beliefs form the strongest linkages when it comes to the discussions of the last days, eschatological events (*al-Ma'ad*) and the future of humans beyond death. Common subjects such as the Last Day or Doomsday, Paradise, Hell, Resurrection and Judgment are descriptively portrayed in sometimes identical images, vocabulary and expressions. This close an affinity means that the Qur'an draws its material from the Pentateuch and the Gospels, as well as Nazarene sectarian traditions. The contents of this chapter will help the reader comprehend the debt that Muhammad owes to Waraqa, the Nosrania who, among other endeavors, translated a Gospel of the Hebrews into Arabic. That Gospel provided Muhammad multiple eschatological issues that are embedded in the Qur'an.

The Secret Appearing of the Last Day

The Qur'an proclaims, "the last hour for this world will come suddenly" (6:31; 7:187). "It will come without any doubt" (6:40; 15:85). "It should come on like greased lightning" (43:66). "Perchance the last hour is nigh" (33:63). In the canonical Matthew context, the Messiah's coming (Gk. *Parousia*) will be sudden "at an unannounced hour" (24:44). "He will arrive unannounced and unexpected" (24:50). He will come "like a thief in the night" (24:43). His presence "is near, even at the doors" (24:33). According to Matthew, the day and the hour, "No one knows, not even the angels of heaven. No, only the Father in heaven knows" (24:36). Paul adds this word about the mystery of Christ's return. "It will all happen in a moment, in a twinkling of an eye" (I Corinthians 15:52).

The Qur'an attests that at the end "the knowledge thereof is with God alone" (43:85). It repeats this assertion several times: "Knowledge is reserved only to God" (7:187). "The knowledge thereof of the moment is by God" (33:63). Even despite his proximity to God, Muhammad himself is not able to know "when this hour will come" (10:48,49). For God "makes none acquainted with his mysteries"(72:26).

The apocalyptic events surrounding the Last Day will be recognized throughout the world. According to the Qur'an on that day the foundations of the earth will change. "The sky is rent asunder" 84:1). "The sky is cleft asunder" (82:1). "The heavens will be unveiled" (81:11). "The sky will be like molten brass" (70:8). "The firmament will be in dreadful commotion" (52:9). It becomes red like ointment (55:37). "The heavens shall be rent asunder like clouds" (25:25).

The more prominent messages about the last day belong to the Meccan revelations of the Qur'an where they are often the only subjects compared to the later Medina Suras which cover many more diverse themes. Judgment Day physical descriptions concentrate on the cosmos. "The sun will be folded up" (81:1), "the moon will be buried in darkness" (75:8); "the moon will be cleft asunder" (54:1); "it will be in her fullness" (84:18). "The sun and the moon will be joined together" (75:9); while "it is not permitted to the sun to catch up the moon or to meet" (36:40). "The stars will fall" (81:2) and "the stars will be scattered" (82: 2). "The oceans will boil over with a swell" (81:6) and "suffered to burst forth" (82:3).

Previous biblical writings, both canonical and non-canonical, have ample texts citing the final day. Beginning with the Old Testament, the prophet Isaiah sees, "The heavens above melting away and disappearing like a rolled up scroll" (Isaiah 34:4). The prophet Joel (2:31) envisions the "moon being red" which is repeated in Acts 2:20 on the Day of Pentecost. In the Jewish inter-testament period, the apocryphal writer Esdras' vision is the moon changing to red color.[1] Another apocryphal text of this period reports, "Both stars, the sun and the moon, will meet together."[2] "The sun will be darkened, the moon will not give light, the stars will fall down from the heavens, and the powers overshadowing the earth will be convulsed" (Matthew 24:29). The non-canonical Apocalypse of John records, "The Rocks will be poured out and flowing down. The doors of the heavens will open and their high walls will be destroyed."[3]

Significant events of the Last Day

The apocalyptic scenes of that final time are never far from the pages of the Qur'an. "Earth will experience a tremendous shaking" (33:11), and "will be shaken to her utmost convulsion" (99:1). "The earth tremors on that great day will be terrible" (22:1). "The earth and the mountains will be in violent commotion. And the mountains will be as a heap of sand poured out and flowing down" (73:14). "On that day earth and heavens will change" (14:48). "The earth will be flattened out" (84:3). "The earth will be moved and its mountains will be crushed to powder in one stroke" (69:14). "On this day, the earth will be rent asunder, from (men) hurrying out" (50:44). "The mountains will be like wool" (70:9), "will fly hither and thither" (52:10), "will be scattered as dust" (77:10), "shall be crumbled to atoms" (56:5), "become as scattered wind" (18:47) and "becoming dust" (56:6).

Sounds of the Last Day

"That day, there will be lightening, thunders and apprehensions" (24:43; 2:20). "The trumpet will sound" (74: 8). "The trumpet will announce the day" (6:73). From the apocryphal Thomas who hears, "That day they will hear a mighty blast in all places... The earth will be rent asunder unexpectedly... It will tremble... Precepts of men will tremble and their eyes will submit."[4]

"There will be famines and earthquakes in many places" (Matthew 24: 7). " Then the Son of Man will appear in heaven, then all of the tribes of earth will mourn" (Matthew 24:30). "He shall send forth his angels with the sound of a mighty trumpet blast" (Matthew 24:31). "The trumpet will blow" (I Corinthians 15:52). "One will hear a soul-stirring" (I Thessalonians 4:16).

"On that day, angels shall be sent down (to men) descending" (in ranks) (25:25), "shall speak to them" (21:103), "shall meet them" (17:93), "shall go in at all doors" (13:23). "God comes with his angels to them in the darkness of thick clouds" (2:210). "The angels will meet together, rank upon rank" (89:22). On Judgment Day, angels will come to testify against people's works. They will accuse them of their misdeeds. Another New Testament epistle forecasts, "See the Lord is coming with millions of his holy ones. He will bring the people of the world before him in judgment to receive their punishments and to prove the terrible things they have done in rebellion against God, revealing all they have said against him" (Jude 14,15).

The foreboding biblical passages have parallel Qur'anic verses that speak about tragic human conditions during the last day. "That day you shall see it, every mother giving suck shall forget her suckling baby, and every pregnant female shall drop her load" (22:2). "Children will become like hoary-headed men" (73:17). "Woe to pregnant women and to those with babies in those days" (Matthew 24:19). "That day shall a man flee from his own brother, his mother, his father, his wife and his children. Each one of them that day, will have enough concern of his own" (80:34-37). "No friend will ask after a friend" (70:10).

Dreadful separation of family members will take place, the Qur'an continues. "That day when no father can avail naught for his son, nor a son avail naught for his father" (31:33). "That day when no protector can avail his client nothing, and no help can they receive" (42:46). "That day when no soul shall have power to do naught for another" (82:19). "Guard yourselves against that day when one soul shall not avail another nor shall intercession be accepted for another" (2:48).

Corresponding to this Qur'anic familial trauma are the Gospel prophecies. "Brother shall betray brother to death and fathers shall betray their own children. And children shall rise against their parents and cause their deaths" (Matthew 10:21). That day nothing can help man other than his good deeds. The Qur'an adds, "For those who respond to their Lord, are all good things. But those who respond not to him, even if they had all that is in the heavens and on earth, and as much more, in vain would they offer it ransom. For them the reckoning will be terrible, their abode will be hell" (13:18).

In Jewish and Christian sources as well as in the Qur'an, material wealth will perish "... They throw away their money. Their gold will have no value in that day of wrath. It will neither satisfy nor feed them, for their love of money is the reason for their sin" (Ezekiel 7: 19). "That day when neither wealth nor sons will avail," adds the Qur'an (26:88). "Some considered multiplicity of wealth and sons as means of salvation. They said, 'We have more in wealth and in sons and we can not be punished'" (34:35). "Your wealth will not help you on Judgment Day" (Proverbs 11:4). "Woe to you, rich people, for you do not remember God when you were rich. You are now ripe for the great day of Judgment," states the Enoch text.[5]

At the end of this momentous day the resurrection will occur and the judgment will start. All the world's people will be present before God, the most just Magistrate. Each individual will bear his deeds in a book. They will be weighed on the just balance. Good people will go on the right of the Lord and evil people on his left. These courtroom provisions are basically the same in the Qur'an as they are in Jewish and Christian books that were available to al-Qiss Waraqa at the time of Muhammad's revelation.

"There will be a separation between good people placed on his right and bad people placed on his left" (56:8-10). A frightful silence will overshadow the entire world before the judgment starts (78:37,38; Revelation 8:1). All works and hidden things will be unveiled (69:18; 18:46) according to record books. "For each of us will give an account of himself before God" (Romans 14:12). The Qur'an continues, "Their tongues, their hands and their feet will bear witness to all that they did" (24:24). "Their ears, their eyes and their skin will bear witness to all what they did" (36:65). Their deeds will be weighed. "He whose balance of good deeds will be found heavy will be in a life of good pleasure and satisfaction. But he, whose balance will be found light, will have his home in a bottomless pit. It is a fire blazing fiercely" (101:6-11).

"And all the nations shall be gathered before him. He will separate the people as a shepherd separates the sheep from the goats, and place the sheep at his right hand and the goats at his left" (Matthew 25:32, 33). Jesus continues his warnings to the disciples about the coming judgment: "He will judge each person according to his deeds" (Matthew 16:27). "Everyone should present his accounts before God" (Revelation 14:12). "The Book of life will be opened. And if any one's name was not found recorded n the Book of Life, he will be thrown into the lake of fire" (Revelation 20:12-15; Daniel 7:10). "All your members will be your witnesses in the eternal house."[6]

St. Ephrem's Vision of Paradise

Much of the afterlife's descriptions found in the Qur'an are close copies of the Christian-Nazarene traditions. However, the two Scriptures depart from each other when the Qur'an draws considerable attention of researchers and common readers alike to the excessive materialism in its description of sensual passions, various food dishes and other enjoyments in the Islamic hereafter. However, some of these bodily pleasures found in the Qur'anic paradise are described by the famous Christian author, Ephrem the Syriac, (d. 379), who is called Chanter of the Holy Spirit. Ephrem's poetical images of paradise include these physical features: "Summit of mountains are under its own. The flood reaches its tiptoes. It covers them and grovels before decreasing, so that it climbs up the mountains and treads on their tops. It kisses the feet of paradise and treads on all heads."[7]

According to the Qur'an, paradise is located in an elevated place above the earth. Good people will stretch themselves "in a garden on a high" (69:22; 88:10), from here they can see perverse people staying behind a barrier below" (7:44).

The surface size of the Qur'anic paradise is unlimited: "Its width is as the width of heaven and earth" (57:21). "A paradise whose width is that of the heavens and of the earth" (3:133). It contains classifications and grades... The believers have grades of dignity with their Lord" (8:4). These grades correspond with a reward system established in the Qur'an. It starts with "the prophet, the sincere, the martyrs and the righteous" (4:69).

The Talmud also provides some details regarding the seven levels of paradise.[8] There are only three heavens according to Ephrem: "The ground floor for penitents, the middle for just people and the higher for meritorious victors and martyrs. The Cupola (Dome) is God's residence."[9] The Apostle Paul recognizes also three levels of heavens (II Corinthians 12:2). At each level, rooms will be available for all groups of the elect. In this connection, the Qur'an supplies, "Those who fear their Lord, will have the lofty mansions, one above another, have been built, beneath them flow rivers of delight" (39:20). The Gospel of John simply quotes Jesus' words, "There are many homes here where my father lives" (John 14:2).

St. Ephrem confirms the existence of only one door. "This door is already opened, and a blessed one is he who goes through... "From now on, take the paradise key for the door smiles at you. The room is well furnished to identify the guests."[10]

The Qur'anic paradise has several doors reserved for God-fearing believers. "Gardens of Eden whose doors will ever be opened to them" (38:50). "Those who feared their Lord will be led to paradise in crowds. Until behold they arrive there, its gates will be opened" (39:73). "The angels shall enter there from every gate" (13:23).

In John's Revelation the Holy City of Jerusalem "has broad and high walls with twelve gates guarded by twelve angels" (Revelation 21:12; Ezekiel 48:30). According to the Talmud, paradise has only two doors.[11] However, this number of doors is not precise in the Testament of Levi.[12] The highest felicity in the Qur'anic and Nazarene paradise lies in the perpetual enjoyment of the Lord's presence, his knowledge and his deep satisfaction regarding believers. This is the great victory: "That day the righteous shall benefit from gardens irrigated by rivers. The Lord will be satisfied from them, and they will be satisfied from Him" (5:119).

Happiness in this world is deceptive compared with the joy waiting beyond the grave. According to the Qur'an, "The hereafter will be better for you than the present. The Lord will give you the best things and you shall be well-pleased" (93:4,5). "Know you all that the life of this world is only play and amusement, pomp and mutual boasting and multiplying (in rivalry) among yourselves riches and children... In the hereafter is a penalty severe, forgiveness from God and his good pleasure. The life of this world is only goods and chattels of deception" (57:20). Jesus admonishes his disciples, "These are earthly treasures that will erode away or may be stolen, whereas the treasures of heaven will never lose their value, and are safe from thieves" (Matthew 6:19).

In his vision of paradise, the saintly Ephrem warns: "Woe unto him who lets lose with hilarity and chattering that day which is opportune for penance,"[13] since "distress will be the reward for laughter."[14] This felicity is for the blessed, exclusively for both adherents of the Qur'an and the earlier Scriptures. The paradise is in the Suras, "the home of peace" (6:127; 10:25) or according to Book of Hebrews, "the place of rest provided by the Lord" (Hebrews 4:1-11). Fear and sadness disappear says the Qur'an, "Enter you here in peace and security" (15:46). "Enter you the Garden: No fear shall be on you, nor shall you grieve" (7:49). Ephrem's fourth century Christian vision of paradise is a place where "tiredness does never exist,"[15] with "irreproachable beauty and impeccable quietude are dwelling there."[16]

According to the Qur'an, the just will never hear lies or idleness in paradise. They will have only peace and quietude. "There will be neither frivolity, nor any taint of ill, only the saying 'Peace, Peace'" (56:26). "Every matter, small and great, is on record" (54:53).

In the Qur'anic paradise there is neither fiery sun nor harsh cold, but "joyful faces" (88:8), "brightening faces" (75:22), "beaming, laughing and rejoicing faces" (80:38,39). "You will recognize in their faces the overcoming brightness of bliss" (83:24). The reason is "they will see neither the sun's excessive heat nor the moon's excessive cold" (76:13). The heavenly people enjoy all things. The Hebrew prophet Isaiah (49:10) says, "The searing sun and scorching desert winds will not reach them anymore." John's Revelation (7:16) adds this description: "They will fully find protection from the scorching noontime heat." Zechariah (14:6) confirms, "On that day, there will be neither cold nor frost. Yet there will be a wonderful day."

Paradise people will sing day and night the praises to the Lord. "They cry with joy: Glory to you, O God! And Peace will be their greeting therein! And the close of their cry will be: Praise be to God, the Cherisher and Sustainer of the Worlds!" (Qur'an 10:10). These praises are an echo to what John records in his book of Revelation (7:9-12). "Salvation comes from our God... Blessing, glory, wisdom, thanksgiving, honor, power and might be to our God forever and forever! Amen!"

Biblical paradise is full of images of water and other liquids that are repeated in Qur'anic images. The following phrase occurs over fifty times. "The just will have gardens beneath which rivers flow" (2:25; 3:15; 4:13; 58:22). There will be, so speaks the Qur'an, four rivers in paradise. "Here is a parable of the garden which the righteous are promised: they are rivers of water incorruptible, rivers of milk which taste never changes, rivers of wine, a joy to those who drink thereof, and rivers of honey, pure and clear" (47:15).

These four rivers are reminders of the four rivers mentioned in the Book of Genesis. "A river from the land of Eden flowed through the garden to water it; afterwards the river divided into four branches: the Pishon, the Gihon, the Tigris and the Euphrates" (Genesis 2:10-14). However, the rivers of the Qur'an will help to improve harvesting of foods (16:65-69) and are more akin to the land promised to the ancient Hebrews. The land will be abundantly supplied with honey, water, milk, oil, corn, barley, wine, figs and grenadine (Deuteronomy 8:7-11). The Talmud promises milk, perfume, honey and wine.[17] In the paradise of Ephrem, one can find wine, milk, honey and cream.[18]

Food in Paradise

St. Ephrem's description: *"The righteous have found the paradise like a kingdom table outstretched before them."*[19] *"It is a banquet of heavenly kingdom, and blessed are those who are worthy to reach it."*[20] *Fruits of all tastes are within reach."*[21]

The Qur'anic food: *"He will provide them with food permanently"* (13:35), *"abundance of fruits"* (43:73; 38:51). *"They shall have fruits, - all they desire"* (56:20). *"There are for them all kinds of fruits"* (47:15). *"The fruits whereof will hang in branches low and near"* (69:23). *"Fruits of trees bend to be picked without pain"* (76:14), in order that *"the person, standing up, sitting or stretching, will be able to pick them,"* according to al-Jalalayn's exegesis.[22]

The Qur'an names the fruits and other foods found in paradise. Most delicious fruits are those from grapevines (78:32), dates and pomegranates (55:68). It includes therein "the most rare flesh of fowls" (56:21; 52:22).

Even in the paradise of Ephrem, wine's quality is as good as that of the wine provided in the Qur'anic paradise. The one who abstains from drinking it in this world, will have it in abundance in the other. "He who, for a reason of asceticism, deprives himself from wine drinking on earth, will see the vine bunches fluttering towards him in paradise."[23] Its quality is like that one of the Talmud wine "the Lord has reserved for mankind since the sixth day of Creation."[24]

The favorite drink in the Qur'anic paradise is wine. It will be drunk from vessels of gold (43:71) and silver and crystal goblets (76:15). The believers drink from cups filled from a delicious white spring. Man's spirit will be neither injured nor elated, as it is with the wine of this world. "In gardens of felicity, ... round will be passed to them a cup from a clear-flowing fountain, crystal-white, of a taste delicious to those who drink thereof, free from heaviness; nor will they suffer intoxication therefrom" (37:44-47). "Round about them will serve young boys of perpetual freshness, with goblets, shining beakers and cups filled from clear-flowing fountains" (56:17,18).

This wine will never lead the righteous to use foolish words nor to perpetuate either sins or lies. "They shall there exchange, one with another, a loving cup free of frivolity, free of all taint of ill" (52:23). It is an exquisite wine of "sealed musk" (83:25). It is "a pure and holy wine" (76:21) "mixed with camphor" (76:5). Wine drinking becomes a licit, legal and honest drink, after having been illegal and prohibited for believers on earth.

The righteous will find rest in the Qur'anic paradise on "elevated seats" (88:13) and "leaning on beds setting orderly" (52:20) while "facing each other" (37:44). "They will be rewarded with the highest place in heaven... Therein they shall be met with salvation and peace" (25:75), inhabiting "lofty mansions built one above another; beneath them flow rivers of delight" (39:20). "Secure they will reside in the dwellings on high" (34:37). "They and their wives will be in groves of cool shade, reclining on thrones" (36:56). "On thrones they will command a sight of all things. On their faces the beaming brightness of bliss will be recognized" (83:23,24). "They will rest on thrones raised high" (56:34). "They will recline on carpets whose inner linings will be of rich, golden brocades" (55:54). The inhabitants of the heavenly abode will be dressed in green, silk and golden garments (18:31; 22:23; 35:33). "They will recline on green cushions and carpets of beauty" (55:76).

According to St. Ephrem, the saved in paradise will enjoy unlimited food, clothes and pleasures. Since Adam and Eve lost their fig leaf garments, those who occupy the New Eden will have their nakedness covered in new white clothes.[25] "They will receive dazzling adornments along with their blessedness."[26] "Men and women will be covered with delightful dresses which screen each of their private parts."[27] Every one of the redeemed "shall cover oneself with light."[28]

These blessed saved, according to Ephrem, "will have banquets in trees in the open air. Flowers will always flourish under their feet. Fruits will float over their heads. Their heavens will be filled with fruits and their earth with flowers... Clouds over their heads will be an umbrella of fruits, and the carpet under their feet a flower-drift."[29] Further the Christian poet Ephrem reports that heaven will provide "holy fruits, delightful adornments, radiant crowns, enjoyments without pain, pleasures without fear as well as eternal wedding festivities."[30]

The prophet Isaiah describes also the inhabitants in the future life:
"My soul shall be joyful in my God:
For he has clothed me with garments of salvation.
He draped about me the robe of righteousness,
I am like a bridegroom in his wedding suit,
Or like a bride with her jewels" (Isaiah 61:10).

The Revelation of John is not unlike the Hebrew poet, Isaiah, and later Christian writer, Ephrem, the Syriac writer, by identifying with the white garments of victory. "The conqueror will be clothed in white" (Revelation 3:5). "The saved will be clothed in white, bearing the palms in the hand" (Revelation 7:9,14). The elders surrounding the throne "will be clothed in white, with golden crowns upon their heads" (Revelation 4:4).

However, included in the Qur'anic paradise, with all of its splendid beauty and the abundance of its pleasures, are the Huriyyat or Huris whom God has specifically created to gratify the righteous who fear him. "We have created the paradise virgins of special creation and made them virgin pure and undefiled" (56:35,36). Whenever a privileged believer in paradise approaches these Huriyyat, they will find their virginity reestablished, as if they were approached for the first time. The Huriyyat will be beloved of their husbands and "equal in age for theirs" (56:37). The fortunate elect will find the *Kawa'ib* (78:33), who are young ladies endowed with well-rounded breasts which incite more and more every day to physical pleasures. With their beauty and charm, they preserve always their chastity. Beside their husbands "they will be chaste women restraining their glances"(37:48). With the permanent brightness of their charm, "they will be like pearls well-guarded" (56:23) and be "like unto rubies and coral" (55:58).

These Huris are compared to "delicate pearls or eggs closely guarded" (37:49). "Neither man nor jinn has ever touched them before" (55:56). "On that day, the companions of the paradise will have joy in abundance. With their wives, they will rest in groves of cool shade, reclining on thrones" (36:55,56). The age of males in paradise, the apocryphal Apocalypse of John states: "They are thirty three years old. All people will have this age on the day of resurrection."[31]

In addition to these female companions, the inhabitants of the Qur'anic paradise, "will be served by young boys of perpetual freshness" (56:17; 76:19), "like pearls well-guarded" (52:24). "If you see them, you would think them scattered pearls" (76:19). Description of these boys, endowed with eternal youth, follows a pattern that is similar to that of Huriyyat.

The paradise of the Qur'an suggests sexual behaviors that some have found to hint of pederasty, conversely, the paradise of Ephrem the Syriac will provide specific spiritual service:

"imparted by breaths of wind which come up in all colors. They bear dishes... Guests will not move from their places... servants will not get tired... Breaths of wind will move before the righteous. One will bring food, the other will pour drinks. Who has never seen these breaths of wind bringing food and drinks? One exhales dews, the other perfume... A rush refreshes, another satiates... One breath ensures the well-being, another the guests' ornaments. One makes fat, another refinement."[32]

While it is impossible to say that Muhammad was aware of all Nazarene descriptions of the paradise, it is apparent that the symbols and images of the previous Scriptures and works of Ephrem were widely spread inside the Nazarene Syriac Church. The Qur'an establishes its own links with the texts of the Syriac Church at the time of Muhammad. Muhammad must have been familiar with the dispersed Syriac Church through his close and personal knowledge with the Nazarene priest, al-Qiss Waraqa Ibn Nawful.

Chapter XIII

Conclusion

This study began with a series of questions about divine revelation that arose out of the study of basic documents of Islam requiring that I scrupulously analyze the Qur'an and the major works of Islamic Hadiths. While there remains many unanswered questions, there is sufficient information to lead me to the pursuit of a remarkable finding. After years of study on the subject of the origin of the Qur'an I can now claim that the teachings of al-Qiss Waraqa Ibn Nawfal, are thoroughly embedded in the Qur'an. This embedding process means that the faith of the early Meccans played a major role in forming Islam as a definite People of the Book who were instructed by this heterodox priest.

Waraqa's diverse ministry includes his selection of his distant cousin, Muhammad, to be his successor as the head of the Nosrania Church, an offshoot of a Jewish-Christian sect. Waraqa's links to the future Arab prophet as part of a master-tutor relationship will have far reaching results, as subsequent history will tell. In all of my research I have come to the conclusion that while the bond between Muhammad, the prophet, and Waraqa could be deemed successful, there came times when the two separated from each other. An obvious separation came at the death of al-Qiss Waraqa when "revelation died" for a number of years. The more serious separation would come later when the Qur'an's final form was promulgated under the rule of the third caliph, 'Uthman, (assassinated 656).

The impact of this final separation is apparent today when fanaticism and militant Islam are still fighting all those who stand for toleration and peace between the followers of Abraham--namely Jews, Christians and Muslims.

Before commenting further on the obvious failures within the Islamic 'Ummah to promote inter-religious peace, I would like to review the successes of the relationship between the priest and the prophet. First of all, in my selection of Qur'anic texts, one is reminded of the extensive similarities of the Qur'an and the previous scriptures. Along with several Old Testament books and the Gospel of the Hebrews and the Jewish Talmud, it becomes evident how much was available to the Arabs in the early seventh century. My hope is that the reader will be convinced as I am that the Qur'an drew its content from these previous sources that ranged from Arab tribal stories to specific Christian authors like the Syrian poet theologian, St. Ephraim.

Another success of the relationship between these two members of the Quraysh clan may be observed in the translation of the Hebrew Gospel into Arabic that would form the basis of the training manual for the struggling monotheistic Hanifi group in Mecca. This became the source for Muhammad's attempts at unifying the various Book People into one organic body which could face the dominating non-believers among the Arabs and non-Arabs. In taking into account this transmission of religious records from one source to another, I reject the foundational doctrine regarding the ultimate source of the Qur'an. Muslims have come to accept as dogma that the Qur'an is tied to a heavenly text, "the preserved table" which came directly to Muhammad, Tanzil, without passing through any other human hands such as described in this text.

The early unity of the various sects who were settled throughout the Hijaz must be considered as a success as well. This unity was based upon equality that declared the new Muslim community equal with the earlier groups who followed the faith of Abraham, Moses and Jesus. The Ebionite priest and the prophet recognized that the origin of disputes dividing orthodox Christians into various denominations like Nestorians, Jacobites, and Nosranians was based upon the nature of Christ and the mystery of the resurrection. It became apparent that the unity of these groups could only be achieved by avoiding the polemics on these theological topics. Unity would be based upon the acceptance of the one God, one book and one people.

Waraqa shared his positive attitudes toward the People of the Book whom he believed were worthy to be emulated because they followed the truth. "They are those who receive God's guidance in the straight path. Follow their guidance" (6:90); "There is among the people of Moses a large number of men who follow the truth as a guide and do justice" (7:159); "Ask the People of the Book, if you do not realize this" (16: 44).

Equality of the People of the Book

"Say: O People of the Book! Come to common terms as between us and you" (3:64).
"We have made it open to all (men) in equality" (22:25).
"They have become equal in that respect" (16:71).
"Your parts are equal" (30:28).
"Every people will be called before its book" (45:28).

Failures of Unity

The attempts at unity following the death of Waraqa led to serious problems with consequences that prevail among Muslims to the present day. The events that followed Muhammad's death in Medina in 632 would disturb the peace of Islam as Muslims made claims and counter claims about who was the proper successor to the Prophet. The community divided into three groups. The first was Shi'a that included the followers of Ali, Muhammad's cousin and son-in-law. A second group followed 'Ubadah al-Khazraji, while a third group chose Abu Bakr who would strengthened his hold on the caliphate during his life.

Other conflicts would follow that widened the jihad attacks on non-believers, the polytheistic Arabs, but soon supplied causes for fighting other Muslims and other Peoples of the Book who were once widely accepted by Muhammad. Now the Jews and the Christians, even the Nosrania believers, were the objects of warfare because they did not accept the "standard" Arab religion.

In this frenzy of religious wars, the Caliph 'Uthman Ibn Affan undertook the challenge to unify the Qur'an which basically revised the early text to fit the needs of the time around the middle of the seventh century. One finds in the 'Uthman version of the Qur'an offensive jihad positions that did not figure in the Muhammadan version that was heavily influenced by Waraqa.

From the beginning of this book, I have maintained that Waraqa and Muhammad worked closely together which means that the Qur'an would favorably represent the Christian/Nosrania sectarian position. There are many verses that show respect for the Christian community as it existed in Mecca. "Truly you will find the Jews and polytheistic Arabs among the strongest in opposition to the believers; And you will find nearest in love to the believers those who say, 'We are Christians;' because among these are those devoted to learning who have given up the world and they are not proud" (5:82).

However, when Muhammad met with a delegation of orthodox Christians shortly before his death, there would be some changes in the Qur'an's attitude toward these who called themselves believers in Christ. Up to that time, the Nosrania believers were accepted as partners with the new Muslims. But when one looks in the Qur'an one soon discovers a whole series of verses that express a grave concern for those who are creating blasphemy by claiming that God has a son. Many of these verses like this one from 17:111 are part of the Meccan revelations when Waraqa played a key role in the life of Muhammad. "Say, 'All praises to God, who has not son and no partner in his kingdom.'"

Several other Suras, which include similar statements that deny that God has a son or partners, come from this early Meccan period (610-622 AD). The list of references includes 10:68; 18:4; 19:35, 88, 91, and 92; 21:26; 23:91; 25: 2; 39:4; 43:81; 72:3; 112:3. All indicate that the injunctions against divine sonship are found in a context that does not fit this specific polemical statement regarding son of God. With the exception of Sura 19, there are no direct references to Jesus' birth within these Meccan Suras.

In a couple of Medina Suras, including some of Sura 19, there are direct references to Jesus, son of Maryam as in 4:171: "O People of the Book! Do not commit excesses in your religion: Nor say anything except the truth about God. Messiah Jesus, the son of Maryam, was no more than a messenger of God...Do not say 'Trinity.' He is above having a son." Another reference to the impossibility of God having children is 6:101. Like the Meccan citations above this verse does not fit the immediate context and is highly likely to be an emendation to the Qur'an of 'Uthman.

A specific Qur'anic reference where the word "Nosrania" (Nasara) appears in Sura 2:135 and following verses. The standard 'Uthmani edition reads, "They say to you: Become Jews- Nasara- and you will be on the straight path.' The word "Nasara" can only be a later addition as the Christians are not a concern here and the word Nasara disturbs the Arabic rhythm of this verse. This sentence originally could be read, "Be Jews, you will be converted." The next verse, 136, reports that Islam is the faith given by Moses and Jesus which is what the Nosrania of Mecca believed and therefore they did not need to be converted. Only the Jews, who are the subjects of this section of the Qur'an, need to be converted (137).

One can discover some of the same editing where the Qur'an speaks clearly in hostile terms regarding the Jews who developed a strong distrust of Muhammad shortly after his arriva in Medina. The 'Uthmani version of Sura 2:113 exclaims, "The Jews say, 'The Christians have nothing firm to stand upon;' And the Christians say, 'The Jews have nothing firm to stand upon' yet they both read the same book."

An earlier citation reads, "And they say: 'None shall enter Paradise, unless he is a Jew or a Christian (Nosrani).' Those are their vain and empty wishes. Say to them: 'Bring your proof if you are truthful'" (2:111). A few verses later, 2:120, the Jews and the Christians are again confronted because they want to convert the Muslims. In each of these verses from Sura 2, the naming of the Jews and the Nosrania in the same message of condemnation reveals a time when the Christians were at war with the Muslims, not at the time of the original Qur'an.

Another example of inserting the Nosrania into a verse that is intended to speak only to the Jews comes with the mentioning of Abraham in 3:67. "Abraham was not a Jew-nor yet a Nosrania-, but he was true in faith, and bowed down his will to God, and he joined not gods with God." The addition of "Nosrania" is superfluous as there was never a claim that Abraham came from a Christian tradition. Rather than assume that the Christians and Jews should be on equal dishonorable footing among Muslims, which is contrary to 5:82 where Christians "are nearest in love" to Muslims, a new reading of 5:51 would be helpful. Simply changing, "do not take Jews and Christians as friends" to read as "Do not take Jews as your friends" brings us closer to the time of the Priest Waraqa and his student, Muhammad.

Finally, any merit of this study lies in the opportunity to celebrate the life of Waraqa who has been blocked out of both Muslim and

Christian understanding of the origins of Islam. My strong desire is to make this Arab Christian more visible even within the context of the Qur'an that has preserved much of his early influence upon his cousin, Muhammad.

Notes

Chapter One

1 Ibn Hisham, *Sirah*, Vol. I, p. 87.

2 Ibn Hisham, p. 115.

3 Nazoraeans were among a number of early Christians throughout the Eastern Empires. Several of these Nazarene sects were closely identified with the early Jewish believers in Jesus. The fourth century Greek writer, Epiphanius, mentions over eighty groups in his list of heresies in *The Panarion*. A new English edtion of this work is published under the name of *The Panarion of Epiphanius of Salamis*, Brill, 1987, p.116.

4 Ibn Sa'ad, *Tabaqat*, p. 66; al-Tabari, *Tarikh*, p. 255.

5 Ibn Qutaybah al-Daynuri, *al-Ma'arif*, p. 640.

6 Al-Balazri, *Ansab*, p. 47; Ibn al-Athir, *al-Kamil fi al-tarikh*, Vol. II, p. 7.

7 Jawad Ali, *Al-mufassal fi tarikh al-'Arab*, Vol. IV, p. 14.

8 Ibn Hisham, *Sirah*, Vol. I, p. 203.

9 Al-Ya'qubi , *Tarikh*, Vol. I, p. 257.

10 Al-Ya'qubi, p. 256.

11 Al-Ya'qubi, p. 254.

12 Al-Azraqi, *Akhbar Makkah*, Vol. I, p. 165.

13 Ibn Qutaybah al-Daynuri, p. 621.

14 Al-Jahiz, *Kitab al-Hayawan*, Vol. VII, p. 216.

15 Al-Ya'qubi, p. 257.

16 Al-Mus'udi, *Muruj al-Zahab*, Vol. II, pp. 108,109.

17 Al-Isfahani, *Kitab al-Aghani*, Vol. III, p. 113.

18 Ibn Sa'd, *Tabaqat*, p. 162.

19 Ibn Hisham, p. 206.

20 Ibn Hisham, p. 206 (note 1).

21 Ibn Hisham, p. 208.

22 Ibn Hisham, pp. 206, 207.

23 Jean Danielou, *Theologie du Judeo-Christianisme*, Paris, 1958, p. 76.

24 Epiphanius, XXX, pp. 3, 13.

25 "Ebion" translated from Hebrew to Greek means "poor."

26 Irenaeus, *Contra the Heresies*, Vol. I. 26.

27 Origen, *Contre Cel*, Vol. II, p. 1.

28 Epiphanius, XXIX, XXX.

29 Eusebius, *Histoire Ecclesiastique*, p. 3.

30 Hippolytus de Rome, Vol. IX, p. 14.

31 Jean Danielou, p. 68.

32 Ibn Hisham, p. 165; Al-Halabi, *al-Sirah al Halabiyya*, Vol. I, p. 130. Al-Halabi (d. 1635) will be further identified by the term "al-Halabiyya" in this work.

33 Al-Halabiyyah, p. 267; *al-Sirah al-Makkiyyah*, Vol. I, p. 130.

34 Al-Halabiyyah, p. 78.

35 Al-Halabiyyah, p. 135.

36 *ALR* and *ALM* are a couple of three Arabic consonants that open eleven of the Qur'an's Suras. These mysterious letters serve some purpose in stressing the importance of the revelations that they introduce. The specific meanings of the three letters have baffled scholars for centuries.

37 St. Jerome, *Commentaire sur Isaie*, Vol. XI, p. 2; *Commentaire sur Matthieu*, Vol. XII, p. 13; *Dialogue contre les Pelagiens*, Vol. III, p. 2.

38 Ignatius of Antiochea, *Smyrnes*, Vol. III, p. 2.

39 Origen, *Commentaire sur Saint Matthieu*, Vol. XV, p. 14; *Commentarire sur Saint Jean*, Vol. II, p. 12.

40 Al-Bukhari (d. 870), *Sahih*, Vol. I p. 38.

41 Al-Halabiyya, p. 274.

42 Al-Halabiyya, p. 274.

43 Al-Halabiyya, p. 274.

44 Al-Bukhari, p. 38.

45 Al-Halabiyya, p. 273.

46 Al-Halabiyya, p. 273.

47 Al-Halabiyya, p. 273.

Chapter Two

1 Ibn Sa'd, *Tabaqat*, Vol. I, p. 119, 156, 168. al-Halabiyya, Vol. I, p. 147.

2 *Al-Sirah Al-Makkiyya*, Vol. I, p. 118; Ibn Sa'd, p. 129; al-Halabiyya, p. 147.

3 Ibn Sa'd, p. 131; al-Halabiyya, p. 152, 153.

4 Al-Halabiyya, p. 155; al-Makkiyah, p. 123.

5 Ibn Hisham, *Sirah,* Vol. I. 194.

6 Ibn Hisham, p. 173; al-Halabiyya, p. 153.

7 Ibn Hisham, p. 174.

8 Ibn Hisham, p. 174.

9 Ibn Sa'd, p. 133; Ibn Hisham, p. 195; al-Halabiyya, p. 155.

10 Ibn Sa'd, p. 131-133.

11 Al-Halabiyya, p. 154.

12 Ibn Sa'd, p. 119, 121.

13 Al-Halabiyya, p. 156.

14 Al-Halabiyya, p. 257, 260.

15 Muslim, *Sahih*, Vol. I, p. 78,79; al-Bukhari, *Sahih*, Vol. I, p. 39; Ibn Sa'd, p. 194.

16 Ibn Hisham, p. 216; al-Halabiyya, p. 258.

17 Al-Halabiyya, p. 259.

18 Ibn Hisham, p. 218; al-Tabari, *Tafsir*, Vol. II, p. 48.

19 *Nihayat al-'Arab*, Vol. XVI, p. 170; Ibn Hisham, p. 219.

20 Al-Halabiyya, p. 259.

21 Al-Halabiyya, p. 259.

22 Al-Halabiyya, p. 260.

23 Al-Halabiyya, p. 259.

24 Ibn Ishaq, in Ibn Hisham. p. 219.

25 Ibn Hisham, p. 219; al-Halabiyya, p. 260.

26 Regarding the state of health that Muhammad was in while he was receiving the revelation, see the following sources: Ibn Hisham, Vol. 1, p. 211; al-Bukhari, Vol. I, p. 23, 31; Muslim, Vol. I, p. 98; Ibn Sa'd, Vol. I, p. 198. al-Halabiyya, Vol. 1, p. 267; al-Makkiyya, Vol. I, p. 183. The subject is covered in numerous other writings as well.

27 Ibn Sa'd, p. 119.

28 Ibn Sa'd.

29 For further study regarding this topic, refer to D. Masson commentary on Sura VI, verse 105 in *Le Coran*, p. 831.

Chapter Three

1 Ibn Hisham, *Sirah,* Vol. I, p. 175; Halabiyyah, Vol. 1, pp. 147-152; *Al-Kamil fi al Tarikh*, Vol. II, p. 39.

2 Ibn Hisham, pp. 175-177; Halabiyyah, p. 151.

3 Al-Halabiyyah, p. 275.

4 Ibn Hisham, p. 221; al-Halabiyya, p. 262; Ibn Sa'ad, Vol. I, p. 195.

5 Ibn Hisham, p. 222; al-Tabari, *Tafsir*, Vol. II, p. 49; al-Halabiyyah, p. 263.

6 Al-Halabiyyah, p. 263,

7 Al-Halabiyyah, p 267; al-Sirah al-Makkiyah, Vol. I, p. 183.

8 Al-Halabiyyah, pp. 275, 276.

9 Al-Halabiyyah, p. 276.

10 Al-Halabiyyah, p. 276.

11 Al-Bukhari, Sahih, Vol. I, p. 18; Muslim, p. 97.

12 Ibn Sa'ad, p. 195; al-Halabiyyah, p. 258.

13 Al-Halabiyyah, p. 258.

14 Ibn Sa'ad, p. 195; al-Tabari, p. 48.

15 Muslim, pp. 97, 98; al-Halabiyyah, p. 267.

16 Al-Halabiyyah, pp. 263, 267.

17 Al-Halabiyyah, p. 269.

18 Al-Halabiyyah, p. 275.

19 Al-Bukhari, Sahih, "Explanation of al-Karamani," Vol. I, p. 38.

20 Ibn Hisham, Vol. II, p. 45,

21 Ibn Hisham, Vol. I, p. 224.

22 Ibn Hisham, Vol. II, pp. 45,46.

23 Sheikh Sobhi al Salih, Mabahith fi al-Qur'an, Beirut, p. 45.
Translator's note: Sobhi was assissinated in Beirut while exiting a mosque in 1986.

24 Mohammad Hussein Haykal, Hiyat Mohammad, ("Life of Mohammad"), Cairo, pp. 135-137.

Chapter Four

1 Muslim, Sahih, Vol. I, pp. 78,79.

2 Al-Bukhari, Sahih, Vol. I, pp. 38,39.

3 Abu Faraj al-Isfahani, Al-Aghani ("The songs"), Vol. I p. 114.

4 Eusebius, Historie Ecclesiastique, Vol. I, p. 22. Note the various names of this Gospel which will be identified either as "Hebrew Gospel" or the "Gospel according to the Hebrews" herein.

5 Eusebius, Vol. III, p. 25.

6 Eusebius, p. 24.

7 Eusebius, Theophanie, Vol. IV, p. 12.

8 Origen, Commentaire sur Saint Matthieu, Vol. XV, p. 14.

9 Origen, Commentaire sur Saint Jean, Vol. II, p. 12.

10 Clement of Alexandria, Stromateis, Vol. II, pp. 9, 45.

11 Epiphanius, *Panarion, XXX*, p. 3. References to this Gospel of Matthew will show that this is not the canonical Gospel of the New Testament.

12 St. Iranaeus, *Contra les heresies*, Vol. 26, 2.

13 St. Jerome, *Commentaire sur Isaie*, Vol. IX, p. 2.

14 St. Jerome, *Commentaire sur Ezekiel*, Vol. XVIII, p. 7.

15 St. Jerome, *Commentaire Ephesians*, Vol. V, pp. 3,4.

16 St. Jerome, *Commentaire sur Matthieu*, Vol. XII, p. 13.

17 St. Jerome, *Dialogue contre les Pelagiens*, Vol. III, p. 2.

18 St. Jerome, *De virus illustrabus*, Vol. II, p. 7.

19 M. J. Lagrange, *L'Evanile selon les Hebreux*, in "Review Biblique," p. 29, 1922.

20 Jawwad Ali, *Al-mufassal fi tarikh al-Arab qabla al-Islam,* ("Details of the history of the Arabs before Islam"), Vol. VI, p. 635.

21 Jean Danielou, *Theologie du Judeo-Christianisme*, Paris, 1958, p. 103.

Chapter Five

1 See also the Qur'an 4:46 where the Jews are cursed for slandering the faith. Muhammad confronted the Jews during his first years in Medina (after 622) when there was constant intrigue and warfare with the Muslims. This culminated in the expulsion of the Jews from that region after the massacre of over six hundred males from the Qurayzah tribe in 626.

2 Theodor Noldeke (1836-1930) as a young German scholar published a text on the origin and composition of the Qur'an. *Geschichte des Qorans* became a foundation document for western understanding of Islam. Richard Bell translated this and added his own critical interpretation of the arrangements of the Suras. Refer to Noldeke article "The Koran" in Ibn Warraq's, *Origins of the Koran*, Prometheus Books, 1998, pp. 36-63.

Chapter Six

1 Al-Halabiyya, Vol. I, p. 37.

2 Al-Azraki, *Akhbar Makka*, Vol. I, p. 37.

3 Al-Ya'qubi, Vol. II, p. 10.

4 Al-Makkiyya, Vol. I, p. 72.

5 Al-Halabiyya, p. 4; al-Makkyya, pp. 22, 23.

6   Ibn Hisham, *Sirah*, Vol. I, p. 43.
7   Al-Halabiyya, p. 4; al-Makkiyya, p. 73.
8   Al-Halabiyya, p. 122; al-Makkiyya, p. 73.
9   Al-Halabiyya, p. 48.
10 Al-Halabiyya, p. 125.
11 Al-Halabiyya, p. 77.
12 Al-Halabiyya, p. 117.
13 Al-Halabiyya, p. 57.
14 Al-Fakhr al-Razi, *Tafsir al-Qur'an*, ("Commentary on Qur'an"), Vol. I, p. 141.
15 Al-Halabiyya, p. 58.
16 Al-Makkiyya, pp. 70-72.
17 Al-Halabiyya, p. 48.
18 Al-Halabiyya, p. 48.
19 Muhammad Abu Hamid al-Ghazali, *Fi fiqh al-sirah* ("On jurisprudence of biography"), p. 67.
20 Ibn Sa'd, Vol. I, p. 120.
21 Ibn Sa'd, p. 122.
22 Al-Halabiyya, p. 125; al-Makkiyya, p. 91.

Chapter Seven
1   Qur'an *hanif* references 2:135; 3:67,95; 4:125; 6:79,161; 10:105; 16:120,123; 22:31; 30:30; 98:5.
2   Al-Tabari, Vol. I, p. 404; al-Alusi, Vol. II, p. 196; Ibn Manzur, *Lisan al-Arab*, Vol. IX, p. 56; al-Tabrasi, Vol. I, p. 467, 215; al-Qartarbi, Vol. III, p. 128; al-Badhawi, Vol. I, p. 159.
3   *Lisan al-Arab*, Vol. IX, p. 51.
4   Al-Tabrasi, Vol. I, p. 515.
5   Ibn Hanbal, Vol. IV, p. 116; Vol. VI, p. 33.
6   *Lisan al-Arab*, Vol. X, p. 402; Zamakhshari, *Al-Kashshaf* ("The Discoverer") Vol. I, p. 178; al-Tabrasi, Vol. I, p. 467.
7   Al-Tabari, Vol. III, p. 105, 306.
8   Al-Zubaydi, *Taj al-Arous* ("The Crown of the Bride"), Vol. VI, p. 77; *Lisan al-Arab*, Vol. IX, p. 56.
9   Al-Qartabi, Vol. IV, p. 109; Ibn Khaldun, Vol. II, p. 707.
10 Al-Tabari, *Tafsir sourat al baqara* ("Commentary on the Second Sura"), Vol. II, p. 135.
11 Ibn Sa'd, Vol. I, p. 2, 55.

12 Al-Mas'udi, Vol. I, p. 78-88.

Chapter Eight
1 The story of the "Seven Sleepers of Ephesus," a fanciful tale that circulating after the fifth century among the Christians, appears as part of Sura 18. The same Sura contains references covering Alexander the Great and extra-biblical topics regarding Moses.
2 Justin Martyr, *Dialogue with Trypho the Jew*, Vol. XXVIII, p. 9.
3 Origen, *Contra Cels*, Vol. V, p. 61.
4 Irenaeus, *Contra les Heresies*, Vol. III, p. 26.
5 Origen, p. 61.
6 Epiphanius, *Panarion*, Vol. XXX, pp. 4,6.
7 Shepherd of Hermas, Vol. IX, p. 12.
8 Irenaeus, pp. 3, 4.
9 *Letter of John*, 9; also *Gospel of Peter*.
10 Irenaeus, Vol. I, p. 24.
11 Irenaeus, Vol. III, p. 33; Vol. V. p. 8.
12 *Protoevangel of James, 1:1.*
13 *Protoevangel of James, 4,5,6.*
14 *Protoevangel of James, 7,8.*
15 *Protoevangel of James, 11.*
16 *Protoevangel of James*, 12-16; *Matthew Apocrypha* 10, 11.
17 Origen, *Commentary on Jeremiah,* Vol. XV, *p. 14.*
18 Jerome, *Commentary on Isaiah*, Vol. XIV, p. 12.
19 Jerome, *Commentary on Micah*, Vol. VII, p. 6.
20 Aphrahate, *al-Bayyinat*, ("The proofs"), Vol. 18:10.

Chapter Nine
1 J. Chanine, *Le Livre de la Genese*, 1945, p. 229.
2 Al-Bukhari, *Sahih*, Vol. 77, p. 13; Muslim, *Sahih*, Vol. II, pp.41,50.
3 Ibn Hanbal, *Musnad*, Vol. V, p. 75.
4 Al-Bukhari, Vol. I, p. 7.
5 Eusebius, *Ecclesiastic History*, Vol. IV, 3-5.
6 Begatti, Marcel, *The Church from the Circumcision*, Jerusalem: Franciscan Press, 1965.
7 Epiphanius, *Panarion*, Vol. XXX, p. 2.
8 Epiphanius, Vol. XXX, p. 17.
9 Irenaeus, *Adv. Omn. Haer.* 5, 1, 3.

10 *Acts of Thomas and Peter*

11 Clement of Alexandria, *Stromateis*, Vol. I. p. 19.

12 Origen, *Commentaire du livre du Levithique*, Vol. VII, p. 2.

13 Acts 15:20,28,29 opens the door for non-Jewish believers in Jesus Christ to enter in full fellowship without becoming Jews. Later some Jewish teachers among the Gentile Christians tried to make the new believers follow the Mosaic law. Paul confronts those who would have the Christians add to their faith in Christ by strict adherence to the Law. See St. Paul's letter to the Galatians.

14 Aphrahate, Vol. XV, p. 7.

15 Epiphanius, Vol. XXX, p. 18.

16 *Kergyme of St. Peter*, Vol. XIX, p. 22.

17 A. Cohen, *Talmud*, Vol. I, p. 5. *Mishnah*, Vol. I. p. 2.

18 *Didache*, Vol. III, p. 3.

19 Hippolytus, *Apostles' Tradition*, 35.

20 Irenaeus, Vol. I, p. 26:2.

21 Cohen, p. 21.

22 Philon, *Laws*, Vol. III, p. 169.

23 *IV Maccabeins, XVIII, p. 7.*

24 *Cohen, p. 211.*

25 Cohen, p. 7.

26 *The Talmud, Yebamot*, Vol. I, p. 44.

27 Abu Daud, *Sunna,* Vol. XIII, p. 3; Ibn Bajah, Vol. X, p. 1.

28 *Kerigyme of Peter, Reconn.*, Vol. I, p. 63.

29 Epiphanius, Vol. XXX, p. 13.

30 Denise Masson, *The Qoran, Comments on Sura V*, verse 115, note 1, p. 826.

31 *Kerigyme of Peter*, pp. 36-39, 55.

32 Al-Azraqi, Vol. I, p. 326.

33 Al-Azraqi, p. 323.

34 Arculfe, who visited the holyland in 670, found a number of baptisteries that bore the images of the prophets Elijah, Moses and Abraham who faced water "crossings." Mary and Jesus appear in all of these ancient images.

Chapter Ten

1 Taha Hussein, *Fi al-adab al Jahili* ("The Jahiliyyah Literature"), 4th Edition, Cairo: Dar al-Ma'arif bi Misr, 1945, p. 78.

2 Taha Hussein, p. 78.

Chapter Eleven

1 IV *Esdras* 7:36; I *Enoch* 54: 1-3.
2 *Babylonian Talmud, Sanhedrin,* 111b.
3 *Babylonian Talmud, Sotah,* 94b.
4 *Babylonian Talmud, Pesahim,* 94b.
5 *Babylonian Talmud, Yebarnot,* 109b.
6 *Babylonian Talmud, Berakot,* 57b.
7 Hippolytus de Rome, *Homelie,* p. 10.
8 Ignace de' Antiohe, *Epitre aux Ephesiens,* p. 5.
9 Cyrille de Jerusalem, *Catechese,* Vol. XVIII, p. 33.
10 A. Cohen, *Le Talmud,* Paris, Payot, p. 449.
11 T. B. Erubin 19a; Cohen, p. 449.
12 Al-Bukhari, *Sahih,* Vol. II, o. 116, note 21.
13 Origen, *Apokatastasis, Denz. Nr.* 211. The Greek word refers to the Acts 3:21 sermon of the Apostle Peter about the "restoration of all things" in the final stages of human history. See John Clark Smith, *The Ancient Wisdom of Origen,* Lewisburg: Bucknell University Press, 1992, p. 36ff.
14 Other New Testament texts used to support a Restoration theory include II Peter 3:13; Matthew 19:28; II Corinthians 5:17.
15 IV *Esdras,* Vol. VII, pp.6-8.
16 I *Enoch,* Vol. XLVI, p. 6.
17 St. Ephrem, *Sermmo alter de Reprehensione,* Vol. II, p. 368. French translation by Lamy. See Sebastian Brock, *The Luminous Eye, the Spiritual Vision of St. Ephrem,* Kalamazoo: Cisterc an Publications, 1985.
18 St. Ephrem, *Le Bapteme du feu,* referenced in C. M. Edsman, p. 131.
19 I *Enoch,* Vol. LXIII, p. 6; XCII, p. 5.
20 I *Enoch,* Vol. LVI, p. 1.
21 *Oracle Sibylline*; St. Ephrem, *Sermmo...p.* 5; *Apocalypse de St. Paul,* Translated by James, p. 554.
22 *The Talmud, Abodah Zara,* 20b; Beresit 6,7. Daniel 13:55 reports the death angel dividing a body in half. This angel appears in the apocryphal characters of Susanna and Daniel.
23 *Midras Tehillim* 52a; *Psaume* XI p. 7.

24 Al-Jalalayn, *Tafsir*, Vol. 79, p. 1.
25 St. Ephrem, Vol. VII, p. 5.
26 I *Enoch*, Vol. LVI, p. 1.
27 *Life of Sant Pachome* (Coptic) from Annales due Musee *Guimet*, 17.
28 Tor Andrae, *Origins of Islam and Christianity*, 1955, p. 67.

Chapter Twelve
[1] IV *Esdras*, Vol. 6, p. 14-26.
[2] *Sibylline Books*, II.
[3] *Apocaplypse of St. John*, 81.
[4] *Apostle of Thomas, Sibylline*, II.
[5] *Enoch*, XCIV, p. 8,9.
[6] A. Cohen, *The Talmud, Ecclesiastes* 4,5, p. 454.
[7] St. Ephrem, the Syriac, *Nashid al-Firdows (Hymn of Paradise)*, Vol. 1, p. 4.
[8] A. Cohen, p. 163.
[9] St. Ephrem, Vol. II, p. 11.
[10] St. Ephrem, Vol VIII, p. 11; Vol. XIII, p. 13.
[11] Cohen, p. 456, 457.
[12] *Testament of Levi*, Vol. XVIII, 10.
[13] St. Ephrem, *Op. Gr.,* p. 2.
[14] St. Ephrem, *Op. Gr.,* p. 3.
[15] St. Ephrem, Vol. I, p. 5.
[16] St. Ephrem, Vol. V, p. 12.
[17] Cohen, p. 420.
[18] St. Ephrem, Vol. X, p. 6.
[19] St. Ephrem, Vol. IX, p. 4.
[20] St. Ephrem, Vol. II, p. 5.
[21] St. Ephrem, Vol. VII, pp. 24, 26.
[22] Al-Jalalayn, *Tafsir al-Qur'an*, Vol. 55, p. 76.
[23] St. Ephrem, Vol. VII, p. 18.
[24] Cohen, p. 420.
[25] St. Ephrem, Vol. VI, p. 9.
[26] St. Ephrem, Vol. VI, p. 18.
[27] St. Ephrem, Vol. VII, p. 5; Vol. IX, p. 28.
[28] St. Ephrem, Vol. VI, p. 23.
[29] St. Ephrem, Vol. IX, p. 5.

[30] St. Ephrem, Vol. XIV, p. 8.

[31] *Apocalypse of St. John*, p. 10.

[32] St. Ephrem, Vol. IX, pp. 6-9, 11.

Biblical References

Selected Bibliography

I- Arabic

Abd al-Baqi, Muhammad, *al-Mu'jam al-mufahras li-alfaz al-Qur'an (Lexicon of Qur'anic terms)*, Dar al-kutub, al-misriya, Cairo, 1960.

al-Alusi, Muhammad Chukri, *Bulugh al-arab fi ma'rifat ahwal al-'Arab (The beginnings of Arabic knowledge)*, Three volumes, al-Rahmaniya, Cairo, 1925.

al-Azraqi, Muhamamd, *Akhbar Makkah wa ma ja'a fiha min athar (Ancient Meccan Antiquities)*, Dar al-Andalus, Beirut, 1978.

al-Baghdadi, Abd al-Qader, *al-Farq bayn al-Firaq (The differences between sects)*, revised by Muhammad M. Abd al-Hamid, Sbayh Bookshop, Cairo, 1964.

al-Balazri, Ahmad b. Yahya, *Ansab al-ashraf (Genealogy of nobility)* Dar al-ma'arif, Le Caire, 1959.

al-Badhawi, Abdallah b. Omar, *Anwar al-tanzil wa asrar al-ta'wi (Clarity of revelation and of interpretation)*, Six volumes, Dar ihya al-turath al-'arabi, Beirut, 1900.

al-Bukhari, Abu 'Abdallah Muhammad, *al-Jami' al-Sajih (the True collection)*, explained by al-Karamani, Four volumes, Dar al-Jil, Beirut, 1967-1971.

al-Ghazali, Abu Hamid Muhammad, *Fi fiqh al-sira (On the jurisprudence of the biography)*, Dar al-kutub al-haditha, Cairo, 1964.

al-Haddad, (al-Ustaz), *al-Qur'an da'wat nassraniyah (The Qur'an, a nazarene vocation)*, Beirut, 1969.

al-Halabi, Ali Burhan al-Din, *al-Sirah al-Halabiyya (the Halabiyya biography)* associated with *al-Sirah al-Makkiya (The Meccan biography)* Ahmad Zayni, a.k.a. Dahlan, al-Istiqamah press, Cairo, 1962.

al-Isfahani, Abu al-Faraj, *Kitab al-Aghani (Book of songs)*, Dar al-kutub al-misriya, Cairo, 1937.

al Jahiz, *Kitab al-Hayawan (Book of Animals)*, Dar al-jil, Beirut, 1973.

al-Jalalayn al-din al-Malalli and Jalal al-din Suyuti, *Tafsir al-Jalalayn (Commentary of the two Jalals)*, al-Mallah, Damascus, 1961.

al-Kitab al-Moqaddass (The Holy Bible), Catholic Press, Beirut, 1975.

al-Mas'udi, 'Ali b. Hussayn, Muruj al-zahab wa ma'adin al-jawhar (Golden meads and jewels), Dar al-Andalus, Beirut, 1973.

al-Nasafi, Abdallah b. Ahmad, Madarik al-tanzil wa haqa'iq al-ta'wil (Understanding of Revelation and exegetical truth), Six volumes, Dar ihya' al-turath al-'arabi, Beirut, 1900.

al-Nisaburi, Muhammad, Ghara'ib al-Qur'an (The secrets of the Qur'an), al-Amiriya Press, Cairo, A.. H.1327.

al-Qurtubi, Muhammad b. Ahmad, al-Jami' li ahkam al-Qur'an (Collection of Qur'anic teachings), Twenty volumes, Dar al-kutub al-misriya, Cairo, 1929-1949.

al-Razi, al-Fakhr, Sharh al-Qur'an (Explanation of the Qur'an), 32 volumes, al-Bahiya, Cairo, 1938 ; Dar al-Fikr, Beirut, 1985.

al-Salih, (Sheikh) Subhi, Mabahith fi 'ulum al-Qur'an (Studies in the Qur'an), Dar al-'Ilm lil-Malayyin, Beirut, 1965.

al-Shahrastani, Abu al-Fath, Kitab al-Milal wal-Nihal (Book of religions and sects), Two volumes, al-Halabi, Cairo, 1961.

al-Tabari, Abu Ja'far, Tarikh al-Rasul wal-Muluk (History of the messenger and kings), Dar al-Ma'arif, Cairo, Eight volumes, 1946-1954.

al-Tabrasi, Ahmad Abu Ali, Majma' al-bayan fi tafsir al-qur'an (Collections of Qur'anic proofs), Dar al-Fikr, Beirut, 1994.

al-Tirmiz, Muhammad b. Issa, al-Jami' al-sahih (The true collection), [Sunan al-tirmizi] al-Babi press, Cairo, 1937.

al-Ya'qubi, Ahmad, Tarikh (History), Two volumes, Dar Sadir, Beirut, n. d.

al-Zamakhshari, Abd al-Qasim, al-Kachchaf an haqa'iq al-tanzil (Discovery of Revelation truth), Four volumes, Dar al-'Ilm lil-Malayyin, Beirut, 1970.

Ali, Jawwad, al-Mufassal fi tarikh al-'Arab qabl al-Islam (Details on the history of Arabs before Islam), 10 volumes, Dar al-'Ilm lil-malayyin, Beirut, 1948-1973.

Chilby, Ahmad, al-Tarikh al-islami wal-hadarah al-islamiya (Islamic and civilization history), Maktabat al-nahdha al-misriya, Cairo, 1970.

Darwaza, Muhammad Izzah, 'Assr al-Nabi wa bi'atuhu qabl al-ba'tha (The Prophet's time and his environment before the mission), Dar al-Yaqzah al-arabiyah, Cairo, 1964.

Haykal, Muhammad Hussein, *Hayat Muhammad (Biography of Muhammad)*, Maktabat al-nahdah al-misriyah, Cairo, 1965.

Hussein, Taha, *Fi al-Adab al-jahili (Jahiliyyah literature)*, Fourth edition Dar al-ma'arif, Cairo, 1947.

Ibn al-Athir, Ali b. Mohammad, *al-Tarikh al-Kamil (The complete history)*, Brill, 1862.

Ibn Hanbal, Ahmad, *al-Musnad (Collection of hadiths)*, Dar al-ma'arif, Cairo, A.H. 1375.

Ibn Hazm, Ali b. Ahmad, *Jawami' al-sira (Collection of biographies)*, Dar al-ma'arif, Cairo, n. d.

Ibn Hishâm, 'Abd al-Malik, *al-Sirah al-Nabawiyyah (Biography of the Prophet)*, 4 volumes, Dar al-Jil, Beirut, 1975.

Ibn Kathir, Isma'il, *al-Sirah al-Nabawiyah (Biography of the Prophet)*, Dar al-kutub al-misriya, Cairo, 1964.

Ibn Qutaybah, Abdallah, *Kitab al-ma'arif (Book of knowledge)*, Dar al-kutub al-misriya, Cairo, 1960.

Ibn Sa'd, Abu 'Abdallah, *Kitab al-Tabaqat al-Kubra (Book of great cultures)*, Two volumes, Dar Sadir, Beirut, 1957-1958.

Karrum, Hasanayn, *Muhammad: Nazra 'assriyya jadida (Muhammad: a modern view)*, Cairo, 1974.

Mar Ephram al-Siryani, *Manzoumat al-firdows (The paradise hymns)*, translated from Aramaic into Arabic by Rufayil Matar & Yuhanna Khawand, (manuscript).

Muslim, Ibn al-Hajjaj, *Sahih (Collection of the hadiths)*, Dar al-Jil, Beirut n.d.[Known as Sahih Muslim]

Nassour, Georges, Translator, *Aqdam al-Noussouss al-Masihiyah (The oldest Christian text)*, Middle East Theological Studies Beirut, n.d.

Qutb, Sayyid, *Fi zilal al-qur'an (In the shadow of the Qur'an)*, Fifth edition, 8 volumes, Dar ihya al-turath al-'arabi, Beirut, 1967.

St. Clair-Tisdall, W., *Tanwir al-afham fi massadir al-Qur'an (The original sources of the Qur'an)*, translated from English into Arabic, Cairo, 1972.

II. English and French

The Holy Bible, French edition published by Jerusalem Bible School and Editions du Cerf, Paris, 1978.

Aigrain, Paul, *Arabie (Arabia)*, a feature article published in: Dictionnaire d'Histoire et de Geographie, Paris, 1974, volume III, column. 1158-1339: [This paper covers the following items : 1. Geography of Arabia; 2. Christian origins in Arabia; 3. Christian populations in Arabia; 4. Christianity in South Arabia; 5. Christians in Mecca].

Amann, E., Apocryphes, in *Societe de la Bible*, Paris, 1959, volume I., column 460-533.

Amiot, F., *La Bible apocryphe*, Evangiles apocryphes, Editions du Cerf, Paris, 1975.

Andrae, Tor, *Les origines de l'islam et le Christianisme*, translated from German into French by Jules Roche, collection, volume VIII, Maisonneuve, Paris, 1955.

--------, *Mahomet : Sa vie et sa doctrine*, Maisonneuve, Paris, 1945.

Begatti, Marcel, *L'Eglise de la Circoncision*, Jerusalem, 1965.

Bell, Richard, *The Origins of Islam in its Christian Environment*, Macmillan, London, 1926.

---------, *Arrangements of the Surahs*, Two Volumes, T & T Clark, Edinburgh, 1937.

Blachère, Régis, *Introduction au Coran*, Maisonneuve, Paris 1947.

--------, *Le Coran*, (translated from Arabic), Maisonneuve & Larose, Paris,1956.

--------, *Le Probleme de Mahomet*, Presses Universitaires de France, Paris,1952.

Bonsirven, J., (ed.) *La Bible apocryphe, en marge de l'Ancien Testament*, Editions du Cerf, Paris,1975 (Selected and translated texts).

Charles, R. H., *The Apocrypha and Pseudepigrafa of the Old Testament*, volume II, London, 1913.

Cohen, A.., *Le Talmud*, (Translated by Jacques Marty), Payot, Paris,1977.

Colon, J.B., *Judéo-chrétiens, in Société de la Bible*, volume IV, column. 1298-1315, Paris, 1960.

Daniélou, Jean, *Theologie du Judeo-christianisme*, Editions du Cerf, Paris,1958.

Huart, Claude, *Une nouvelle source du Coran*, in *Journal Asiastique*, IV(1904), p.126-129.

Ibn Ishaq, *The Life of Muhammad*, Translated by Alfred Guilaume, Oxford, 1955.

Ibn Warraq, *The Origins of the Koran*, Prometheus Books, Amherst, NY, 1998.

James, M.R., *The Apocryphal New Testament*, London, 1953.

Lagrange, M. J., *L'Evangile selon les Hébreux*, in *Revue Biblique*, 2(1922) p.161-181; 3(1923) p. 322-349.

Lammens, Henri, *Makka (Mecca)*, in Encyclopédie de l'Islam, volume III, p.509.

--------, *L'age de Mahomet et la chronologie de la Sira*, in *Journal Asiatique*, XVII (1911), p. 201-234.

--------, *Qoran et Tradition. Comment fut composée la vie de Mahomet*, in *Recherches des sciences Religieuses*, I(1910), p. 35-68.

Marchal, L., *Judéo-chrétiens*, in *Dictionnaire de théologie catholique*, Paris, 1975, volume VIII.

Masson, Denise, *Le Coran, Inroduction, traduction et notes*, Bibliothèque de la Pléiade, Paris,1967.

--------, *Monothéisme coranique et monothéisme biblique*. Doctrines comparées, Desclée de Brouwer, Paris 1976.

Prat, F., *Judaïsants et Judéo-chrétiens*, in *Dictionnaire Biblique*, volume.III., column 344-348.

Ryckmans, C., *Les religions arabes préislamiques*, in Mortier-Gorce (ed.), *Histoire des religions*, volume III, Paris, 1947, p. 315-332.

Vigouroux, F., *Evangile des Hébreux*, in *Dictionnaire Biblique*, volume III, column 552-554.

Watt, W. M., *Mahomet à la Mecque*, translated by Douveil, Paris 1956.

---------, *Mahomet à Médine*, translated by Guillemin et Vaudou, Paris 1959.

Zakarias, Hanna, *L'Islam: entreprise juive de Moïse à Mohammad*, Editions du Scorpion, Four volumes, Paris, 1955.

Index

A

Abraham, 2, 22, 24, 49, 51, 55, 61, 67- 69, 71, 81, 84, 120, 139
Abd al-Muttalib, 1, 5, 11, 13, 21, 61
Abd al-Uzzah, 1, 2 ,4, 6
Abu Bakr, 29, 33, 137
Abu Talib, 17-20, 26, 29, 37, 64
Acts of Thomas, 93
Adam, 2, 38, 81, 84, 132
Aishah, 21
Al-Azraqi, 4, 61, 99
Al-Bukhari, 11,13,14, 22, 41, 92
Ali, 2, 26, 36, 100, 137
Aphrahate, 89, 94
Al-Qibla, 96
Al-Yaqubi, 4, 22, 61, 89
Arabic, 12, 13, 38, 44-50, 56
Aramaic, 12, 41, 42

B

Bridesmaids Parable, 110, 117
Buhayre, Bahira, 11, 29, 38, 73
Byzantines, 3, 6

C

Cerinthism, 9
Christians 2, 4, 11, 14, 23, 59, 61, 70, 75-79, 95,148 (Ch 9, no. 13)
  Cf. Nosrania, Rituals, Chr stian, Najran, Trinity, Jesus Christ
Christian Fathers, 8-12, 22, 31, 41-43, 92, 93, 114
Circumcision, 7, 73, 91, 92
Clement of Alexandria, 42, 93
Cyril of Jerusalem, 114